50 things you want to know about world issues...

but were too afraid to ask

50 things you want to know about world issues...
but were too afraid to ask

KEITH SUTER

BANTAM
SYDNEY AUCKLAND TORONTO NEW YORK LONDON

50 THINGS YOU WANT TO KNOW ABOUT WORLD ISSUES . . .
BUT WERE TOO AFRAID TO ASK
A BANTAM BOOK

First published in Australia and New Zealand in 2005
by Bantam

Copyright © Keith Suter, 2005

All rights reserved. No part of this publication may be reproduced, stored in a retrieval system, transmitted in any form or by any means, electronic, mechanical, photocopying, recording or otherwise, without the prior written permission of the publisher.

National Library of Australia
Cataloguing-in-Publication Entry

>   Suter, Keith D.
>   50 things you want to know about world issues . . .
>   but were too afraid to ask
>
>   ISBN 978 1 86325 503 5.
>   ISBN 1 86325 503 6.
>
>   1. World politics. 2. International relations. I. Title.
>
>   327.1

Transworld Publishers,
a division of Random House Australia Pty Ltd
20 Alfred Street, Milsons Point, NSW 2061
http://www.randomhouse.com.au

Random House New Zealand Limited
18 Poland Road, Glenfield, Auckland

Transworld Publishers,
a division of The Random House Group Ltd
61-63 Uxbridge Road, Ealing, London W5 5SA

Random House Inc
1745 Broadway, New York, New York 10036

Front cover illustration of hand courtesy of Getty Images
Cover design by Darian Causby/www.highway51.com.au
Typeset in 10.5pt Sabon by Letter Spaced
Printed and bound by Griffin Press, South Australia

10 9 8

Contents

Introduction ... 1

1 How many countries are there in the world and how are they created? ... 3
2 Can the west win the War on Terrorism? ... 10
3 What else could the US have done after September 11? ... 19
4 Are humans warlike by nature? ... 22
5 What is the risk of a World War III? ... 25
6 Should Third World debt be forgiven? ... 37
7 What is the McDonald's Golden Arches Theory of World Peace? ... 44
8 Should New Zealand merge with Australia? ... 51
9 Why did the US invade Iraq? ... 54
10 What is 'globalisation'? ... 71
11 Is globalisation good or bad? ... 78
12 Why are African children starving? ... 84
13 Why is Australia the US's most faithful ally? ... 88
14 What are the disadvantages of Australia's traditional foreign and defence policy? ... 96
15 Is the United Nations a world government? ... 98

16	Why doesn't the UN do more?	104
17	Will there ever be peace in Israel/Palestine?	109
18	Is Microsoft more powerful than, say, Poland?	118
19	What is 'blow-back' and how is it significant in US foreign policy?	120
20	What are rogue states?	123
21	Is the Russian empire likely to break up?	128
22	Should Australia accept more refugees?	138
23	What is microcredit and how is it changing the lives of women in Bangladesh?	145
24	Is the world running out of oil?	149
25	Is the world running out of water?	157
26	Will the US end up as just another tourist attraction?	160
27	What is the impact of the mass media on international politics?	165
28	How easy is it for governments to control the spread of information?	173
29	Is Taiwan a country?	177
30	Will Australia ever introduce an Australia Card?	181
31	What is the relationship between Australia and the UK?	183
32	What is 'free trade'?	189
33	Does Australia win or lose from free trade?	194

34	Why is Indonesia the 'crippled giant' of South East Asia?	198
35	Are environmental problems a threat to world peace?	208
36	What are 'green taxes'?	218
37	Who owns the South Pole?	222
38	Can democracy be exported?	230
39	Can democracy take root in Arab societies?	237
40	Will the US succeed in making Iraq a democracy?	240
41	Is foreign aid a waste of money?	242
42	Is Islam a threat to world peace?	248
43	What are the threats to Islam?	255
44	What are 'human rights'?	260
45	What progress has been made in the international protection of human rights?	269
46	How serious is the US's national debt problem?	273
47	What is the 'Fourth World'?	278
48	Which country is likely to replace the US as the next superpower?	281
49	What is 'citizenship'?	283
50	How does Australia rank internationally in terms of the 'good life'?	286

| Acknowledgements | 295 |

Introduction

These days we are deluged with information about world affairs. All the great improvements in communications have meant that we can learn more about the world, in less time than ever before.

The problem now is not information, but making sense of it all. This means trying to see the underlying patterns. Events do not just happen one after another: there is often a theme or two behind them. Political miscalculation, war, greed, stupidity are unfortunate common characteristics throughout history, although of course there are positive themes as well.

Meanwhile, there are really substantial changes also taking place that are unprecedented. For example, there is the impact of globalisation, which is the biggest change to the international order for 350 years. We have embarked on a journey to an unknown destination. No one knows for sure what the world will look like in, say, fifty years, and to what extent it will have changed.

The purpose of this book is to provide capsule commentaries on what is taking place internationally. The fifty questions are derived from the major issues that have arisen over the years on my Channel 7 *Sunrise* segments and interviews on Sky TV, Radio 2GB and ABC Radio.

The answers are based on three factors: putting the question into context to provide a sense of history, analysing the current situation, and suggesting how the situation may evolve. I hope that with this book in hand you will be better able to make sense of the complicated world that we live in and make your own decisions about current issues.

1

❓ How many countries are there in the world and how are they created?

I am often asked this question and it is a great basis for understanding world affairs. There are about 200 countries in the world. The 191 that belong to the United Nations are known as nation-states. The rest are micro-states and have a population smaller than that of inner Sydney.

The creation of nation-states was a deliberate process that began some centuries ago in Europe. Rulers needed to consolidate themselves against domestic and foreign forces. In order to subdue what was a patchwork quilt of barons and other localised authorities, they created what we now call the early monarchies – such as those in England and France. Some of the monarchies eventually became republics, but they all shared a common characteristic: a strong central national government to run their affairs. This European system of government was eventually taken around the world and is now the international norm.

The government had to manufacture loyalty to the nation-state and so each country over time evolved a series of symbols to reinforce the people's consciousness of their national identity: a flag, an anthem, historical figures and events, special holidays. Schoolchildren studied universal subjects such as mathematics, science and geography, but other elements in the curriculum – especially history – took on a national focus, just as teaching itself followed a national pattern. Gradually, there came to be one national language for a country.

The creation of a national identity was necessary to underpin foreign policy: it constituted the distinction between the 'national community', which the government represented abroad, and the foreigners it dealt with. Over the centuries, as governments have required more and more from their citizens – such as taxes and conscripts – they've had to work harder at creating a sense of national identity.

The process of European colonisation

Europe has dominated the globe for five centuries. The process of colonisation began around AD1500, when Europeans started sailing to every part of the world in search of gold, silver, spices and other commodities. Spain and Portugal – two of Europe's oldest nation-states – were first to venture forth, followed by other nation-states such as the Netherlands, France, Britain, Belgium, Italy and Germany.

The exploitation of Africa offered the colonisers the opportunity to set up a triangle of trade: European-manufactured goods were used to buy African slaves from Arab slave traders; the slaves – more than 11 million people – were shipped across the Atlantic to the Americas, where they worked on sugar, cotton and tobacco plantations, the produce of which was shipped to Europe. People wishing to escape persecution in Europe also fled to the Americas, where they took over parts of the land. Australia, too, was colonised and became a dumping ground for British convicts. There were various motives for colonisation, but the overall effect was that thriving indigenous civilisations were destroyed and European citizens and values were imposed on the land.

Colonialism not only destroyed civilisations, it also transported rivalries between the colonial powers to other parts of the globe. The victims of colonialism were drawn into struggles they knew nothing about and were often recruited into European forces to fight for European causes – such as Indian forces fighting for the UK in World War I and World War II.

Colonialism had its critics even at the height of imperialism a century ago: they argued that it was wrong for one country to dominate another. These critical voices grew much louder during World War I, which was blamed partly on competing colonial ambitions between Germany and other great powers. After the war, Allied countries agreed – for one of the few times in history – that the victorious countries should not take over the territories of the defeated countries. Instead, they should be held in trust, called a 'mandate', to be put on the road to independence. This work was overseen by the League of Nations.

At the end of World War II, the same agreement was made – this time under the aegis of the United Nations (which replaced the League of Nations). Australia, for example, had acquired German New Guinea as a League Mandate Territory and after the war this became a UN Trust Territory. Australia administered it with its own colony of Papua until 1975, when the nation-state of Papua New Guinea received its independence.

The process didn't just affect the Trust territories of the defeated countries; the Allied countries also had to grant independence to their own extensive colonies.

The end of the European empires

In 1945, the UN had only 51 members, but the winding up of the European colonies after World War II more than tripled this number.

This transformation – one of the greatest changes of the twentieth century – occurred for four reasons:

1. Colonial peoples rebelled against their masters. They were partly inspired by Japan's entry into World War II when it had some early victories against western countries. Japan may have eventually lost the war, but its initial successes – especially the capture of Singapore in 1942 – showed that Europeans were not invincible.
2. The global communications revolution – then in its early stages – enabled the worldwide broadcast of ideas about resisting colonialism. India's non-violent resistance to British rule received much sympathetic coverage in the US. The US had worked with the UK to end German and Japanese aggression but now found itself linked with an old-style colonial power. India's independence created a precedent for other colonies.
3. Colonial powers had been weakened by the fighting among themselves. The UK, for example, emerged

from World War II heavily in debt and unable to maintain the large military force required to put down colonial rebellions. The US, which had finished the war as the world's richest country, was unwilling to provide money to maintain old European empires and wanted them wound up.

4. The times had changed. Even in Europe there was less enthusiasm for maintaining the burden of empire. Economists argued they had made all the money they could from colonies and that continued imperialism would be a financial burden. One motivation for imperialism had been to make as much money as possible in as little time as possible, with little regard for the colonial peoples. Now empires were said to be ways of introducing 'civilisation' to people, which would require schools, roads and hospitals – the cost of which would far exceed the money to be made out of maintaining the empire.

The United Nations itself is the best example of how attitudes have changed. Initially, its membership largely comprised developed countries, with only two black African member-states: Liberia and Ethiopia. Gradually, as the colonial empires were wound up, the new countries joined the UN. That formal process is virtually complete. Most of the territories that retain some form of colonial status have very small populations.

The permanent impact of Europeanisation

For better or worse, the world has been permanently transformed by 500 years of Europeanisation. Tribal peoples have had their lands divided and conquered, and descendants of Europeans now live in all parts of the globe. European cultures now dominate the world, such as the prevalence of the English, French and Spanish languages. But countries cannot be 'ethnically cleansed' to revert back to their 'ethnically pure' condition – though some appalling attempts are being made.

In 1993, I attended a Club of Rome conference in Hanover, Germany, where there was a discussion about how to define 'Europe', especially in the context of the enlargement of the European Union (formerly called the European Community). One speaker asked whether Canada was more 'European' (thanks to the British and French) than Albania, say, or whether Brazil was more 'European' (thanks to Portugal) than Bulgaria. 'Europe' is defined by its political borders. But its cultural impact is felt around the world. Indeed, the most distant part of 'Europe' is to the east of Australia: the former French territories in the South Pacific that are part of the European Union.

From about 1500, Europe was a continent of emigrants. The global Europeanisation process involved the mass transfer of people to the rest of the world. Today, Europe is a continent of immigrants. People move to Europe in the hope of a better life – especially people from the ex-colonies – or go there as overseas students to get a better education and then inter-marry and stay.

People move to new countries to seek employment, or are recruited by countries with a labour shortage. Melbourne is the third-largest Greek city and more Maltese live in Australia than in Malta.

Transnational corporations have contributed to this process by transferring staff overseas to work in branch offices. These people sometimes then stay on. Similarly some staff and volunteers from non-governmental organisations have remained in the countries they have been sent to work in.

Some of the new governments in the former Soviet republics would like to remove the Russians who live there, but the Russians – many of whom were sent there by Moscow against their will – have now settled in the republics, intermarrying and forming new relationships, and have no families to return to in Russia.

The Iron Curtain may have come down, but the west Europeans – and US, Canada and Australia – have installed a 'Glass Curtain', as I talk about later in 'Should Australia accept more refugees?'. Thanks to the mass media revolution, people in Third World countries can see on television the better lifestyles available in the west, but they are denied entry to those countries.

Although the process of European colonisation has ended, we will be living with its consequences indefinitely.

Could more countries be created?

Yes, more countries could be created. Palestine is likely to be the next new country – if President Bush's 'road map for peace' is successful. There is also the possibility that Russia could fragment: Chechnya might break away, for example. Indonesia could also break up: we might one day see the creation of an independent Aceh. And some human rights activists would like Tibet to be independent of China.

2

? Can the west win the War on Terrorism?

The first conflict of the twenty-first century has been fought with techniques much like those of the previous century. It remains to be seen how successful the US's grand strategy will be against the al-Qai'da network.

I was opposed to the US attack on Afghanistan in 2001, because I thought that anyone smart enough to plan the September 11 attacks would have also factored in a US military retaliation. Terrorism is partly designed to provoke a harsh response by a government, so that (in theory) the resulting oppression will lead to a public backlash in favour of the terrorist organisation's political aims. (Personally, I'm sceptical of the theory but that's a reason given for terrorism.) Osama bin Laden may well have created an ambush that the Americans have walked into.

Four years on, the US and its allies are still bogged down in Afghanistan, and bin Laden – who may be dead or alive – is still a hero to many alienated young Muslims. He has long stopped being the military strategist; he's now the spiritual inspiration. Just as the conflict in Northern Ireland has lasted for over thirty years, in theory this war could go on for that long too.

The War on Terrorism is a war on a form of warfare. It's a meaningless term, used for glib media purposes. President Bush should have called it a policing action rather than a 'war', and he should have been specific about the target.

The phrase 'War on Terrorism' has four major problems:

1. There is no agreed definition of 'terrorism'.
2. Governments aren't consistent in how they deal with terrorism.
3. Not all terrorism is carried out by non-governmental organisations.
4. Previous attempts to outlaw international terrorism have failed.

There is no agreed definition of 'terrorism'

The practical problem with defining terrorism is that one government's terrorist is another's freedom fighter. Indeed, it is possible for a person to move from terrorist to freedom fighter and even to the head of government. For example, Nelson Mandela was regarded by the South African Government as a terrorist and was held in prison throughout the 1960s to late 1980s. When there was a change in the political circumstances, he was released from prison and went on to become South Africa's first black president.

In 1947, the Jewish Irgun group fought against the British for the creation of an independent Israeli state. The British considered it a terrorist group, but its leader, Menachem Begin, later became Prime Minister of Israel. Indeed, many of the first generation of leaders of the new countries created out of the former British and French colonies had served time in prison or had been on the run for offences that their colonial masters regarded as terrorism. Even George Washington, between 1776 and 1783, might have been called a terrorist. 'Terrorism' is a pejorative, politically coloured phrase devoid of legal meaning.

It also contains the implication that the victims are innocent and unarmed – as distinct from combatants taking part in an armed conflict. But about 90 per cent of the victims of modern conflict are civilians. Indeed, in percentage terms, even more journalists are killed in conflict than civilians. In the current era of warfare, then, soldiers and other military personnel have – in percentage terms – a low rate of casualties.

Governments are not consistent in how they deal with terrorism

The lack of a generally accepted definition helps explain the inconsistent pattern of government practice regarding terrorism. A good example of this was the government response to the first major aerial hijackings carried out by East Europeans fleeing Communism in the early years of the Cold War after 1945. The hijackers stole aircraft to land in Western Europe, usually West Germany. These people were seen as heroes in western countries and weren't returned to their Communist rulers – as the Communist governments demanded. Western countries only began to regard aerial hijacking as a crime when their own aircraft were being used.

The 1963 Convention on Offences and Certain Other Acts Committed on Board Aircraft (the 'Tokyo Convention') dealt with the safety of aircraft and maintenance of order on board. However, the problem of unlawful seizure was considered only in Articles 11 and 13 and there was no obligation on the governments that had agreed to the treaty to prosecute or extradite the alleged offender. Their duty concerned only the release and safe return of the crew, passengers, aircraft and cargo.

In the late 1960s, the hijacking of aircraft for political motives – as distinct from asylum seekers fleeing from governments – became more widespread, particularly against western governments. The 1970 Convention for the Suppression of Unlawful Seizure of Aircraft (the 'Hague Convention') goes considerably further than the Tokyo Convention and deals explicitly with aerial hijacking. This was followed by the 1971 Convention for the Suppression of Unlawful Acts Against the Safety of Civil Aviation (the 'Montreal Convention'), which protects civilian aircraft from attack and obliges governments that accept the treaty to work together to punish hijackers. There was also the 1988 Protocol on the Suppression of Unlawful Acts at Airports Serving International Civil Aviation, which added to the definition of 'offence' given in the Montreal Convention. Taken together, these treaties represented a very different attitude towards aerial hijacking than the cavalier approach of western countries during the early Cold War years.

However, the September 11 tragedy showed that aerial hijacking is still possible, irrespective of the considerably increased range of treaties and airport security. This is a problem for all legal systems, of course. For example, all countries have laws against murder but murder is still committed.

Another example of inconsistency is the current round of conflict in Northern Ireland, which began in the late 1960s. British politicians complained about the way elements in the US – such as the legal system and non-governmental fundraising – assisted the Irish Republican Army (IRA). The US refused to extradite alleged IRA members because at that time the US didn't regard them as terrorists.

In 1996, the US began designating certain organisations as Foreign Terrorist Organizations (FTOs). They passed the Antiterrorism and Effective Death Penalty Act, which made it illegal for persons in the US or subject to US jurisdiction to provide material support to FTOs; required US financial institutions to block assets held by FTOs; and enabled the US Government to deny visas to representatives of FTOs. The October 2001 list identified twenty-eight FTOs, with the breakaway faction Real IRA listed, rather than the 'real' IRA. Given the amount of assistance the conflict in Northern Ireland has received from persons and organisations based in the US (as distinct from official government sources), this process is too little too late.

Not all terrorism is carried out by non-governmental organisations

Another problem is that the word 'terrorism' is usually applied only to non-governmental organisations – Osama bin Laden's al-Qai'da network, for example, or the IRA, or the Tamil Tigers in Sri Lanka. This approach ignores the role of governments. It perceives terrorism as what is done *to* a government, not *by* it.

It could be argued, however, that the worst terrorists in the twentieth century were all recognised leaders of government: Stalin, Hitler, Mao Zedong and Pol Pot. These leaders killed many of their own people through various 'purges', most of them innocent victims rather than armed opponents of the regime. In almost all cases, the victims were killed in appalling circumstances with no adequate trial. They were simply in the wrong place at the wrong time or had the wrong economic, social, ethnic or religious background.

Similarly, a number of regimes in the post-World War II era used 'terrorism' – according to the definition of some people – on their own citizens and were supported in this by the US. For example, Chile was one of the few countries (possibly the only one) in Latin America with an established tradition of democracy. President Salvador Allende was elected in 1970 and instituted a program of socialist reforms. The US Government, under President Richard Nixon, retaliated with a destabilisation program. General Augusto Pinochet led a military takeover on 11 September 1973 to stop the reforms and President Allende was killed in the military coup. The military then cracked down on its opponents. After his retirement, Pinochet was arrested in the UK in October 1998 on a Spanish warrant for offences committed against Spanish citizens during his time in power. The general eventually returned to Chile. Some have claimed that Henry Kissinger, who was US Secretary of State at the time of the Chile tragedy, should be vulnerable to a similar indictment as one of the chief architects of the destabilisation program.

The destruction of the Greenpeace vessel, *Rainbow Warrior*, is another good example of both state terrorism and inconsistent government practice. The vessel, which had been campaigning against French nuclear testing in the South

Pacific, was destroyed in Auckland Harbour on 10 July 1985 by members of the French secret service, the Direction Générale de Sécurité Extérieure (DGSE). Forty kilos of explosive were used to sink the ship, also killing one crew member. All but two of the French agents escaped back to France. The two who were caught on 12 July pleaded guilty on 4 November 1985 to the lesser charge of manslaughter rather than murder. They were each sentenced to ten years in a New Zealand prison.

The New Zealand Government was subjected to considerable pressure by France to release the agents immediately. Eventually, the UN Secretary-General provided a mediation of the dispute by which the agents were transferred to serve their term in a French prison (from which they were released prematurely), with the payment of compensation to New Zealand by France. In July 1991, one of the agents received a French decoration.

Not even the French Government denied that French agents destroyed the *Rainbow Warrior*, but there remains a lack of clarity as to why they did it (because the vessel had also been monitoring the impact of US nuclear tests three decades earlier in Micronesia) and who in Paris authorised the attack. Given the amount of resources involved, this was more than just a few agents operating on their own initiative. Meanwhile, the word 'terrorist' was never used by France's allies – who were also supposed to be New Zealand's allies – to describe this attack.

New Zealanders were angered by the lack of support from their erstwhile allies, not least the UK, where the *Rainbow Warrior*, formerly the *Sir William Hardy*, a British fisheries research vessel, was registered. At the time of the attack, New Zealand, with David Lange as prime minister, was an outspoken critic of the nuclear arms race and had alienated itself from the US and Australia, which led to the suspension of the Australia New Zealand United States (ANZUS) defence alliance. Therefore, the UK, US and Australia decided not to assist New Zealand over the *Rainbow Warrior* tragedy and refused to regard France as a 'rogue state'.

Previous attempts to outlaw international terrorism have failed

History contains a bad omen for the creation of international treaties against terrorism.

The first international treaty on terrorism arose out of the assassination of King Alexander of Yugoslavia in October 1934. Hitler came to power in Germany in 1933 and France was positioning itself vis-à-vis Hitler and Mussolini in Italy. King Alexander had been invited to France by the French Foreign Minister, Louis Barthou, as part of France's plan to improve its strategic situation in the Balkans. In Marseilles, a Macedonian revolutionary incited by a fanatical group of Croatians assassinated the King, and Barthou was struck at the same time. The assassination was caught on news film and so was well publicised by the media standards of the day. It was one of the most appalling events of the inter-war period, and was most embarrassing to France which had been unable to protect its royal visitor.

In 1934, the League of Nations Council – the forerunner of the United Nations Security Council – took steps to prepare an international convention for the prevention and punishment of acts of political terrorism. The initial proposal was made by France, concerned by the King's assassination. The Council took the view that nation-states had a duty to suppress terrorist activity and to comply with any request for help in putting down adventurers foregathering within their jurisdiction.

A treaty was adopted at Geneva in November 1937: the League of Nations Convention for the Prevention and Punishment of Terrorism. Under this treaty the contracting states agreed to treat acts of terrorism as criminal offences, including conspiracy, incitement and participation in such acts, and, in some cases, to grant extradition for such crimes. However, only one country ratified the treaty – India, which was facing a great deal of violence at the time – and so it never came into force.

The reality is that terrorism can take place no matter what arrangements are made to outlaw it. At the personal level, it's important to note that the object of terrorism is to terrorise; if you're terrified, then the terrorist has won. People who cancel their travel plans for fear of terrorism, for example, are giving in to terrorists. As Winston Churchill said at the height of the German bombing Blitz on London on 14 July 1941: 'You do your worst – and we will do our best'. Terrorism can be reduced but it can't be eliminated.

The British reaction to the July 2005 terrorist strike on London showed the country's capacity to handle such attacks. London was first bombed ninety years ago by World War I German Zeppelins, and in more recent years London has been attacked by the IRA and anarchist groups such as the Angry Brigade. There was therefore an institutional memory ready to cope with the July 2005 attacks – people knew instinctively what to do and not to panic. They took the events in their stride. 'Resilience' is a key factor – it may not be possible to stop the attacks but the carnage can be limited by the right response.

3

❓ What else could the United States have done after September 11?

Al-Qai'da must have known the US would quickly track them down after the September 11 terrorist attacks, and must have factored the US military response into their planning from the outset. This leads us to the questions: is the US military campaign actually fighting to an agenda drawn up by Osama bin Laden? Has the US been led into an ambush of sorts? When we see how the US and its allies are still bogged down in Afghanistan, we might answer 'yes'.

So what could the US have done instead? An alternative grand strategy might have focused on denying the terrorists the opportunity for martyrdom status in many developing countries that dislike US economic and foreign policy.

First, the US could have said that it wouldn't attack Afghanistan because the Afghanis had already suffered so much from the 1979 Soviet invasion and subsequent civil wars and drought. Instead, the US could have provided extensive amounts of foreign aid to Afghanistan, in a hearts-and-minds campaign to win over Afghanis and others in the Islamic world. This would have neutralised the 'Islamic factor' by showing a Christian country generously assisting one of the world's poorest nations.

Second, the US could have offered a substantial reward (say US$500 million) to entice groups such as the Russian Mafia – or even the Taliban – to hand over Osama bin Laden dead or alive. Half a billion dollars sounds a large sum of money, but it's less than the cost of a bomber. The US believes in capitalistic incentives – why not use the market to encourage people to find Osama bin Laden? By this time ordinary Afghanis would be pro-American because of the aid and so could have helped in the search.

Third, the US could have created an international tribunal to try Osama bin Laden, if he were captured alive. This would have emphasised the importance of the international rule of law.

Finally, President Bush could have used the national sense of crisis generated by the September 11 attacks to launch a campaign for energy independence, to reduce US reliance on imported oil. This could have included encouraging the manufacture of smaller vehicles, the development of transport habits that involve fewer cars, and the creation of alternative energy sources.

It is true that this alternative grand strategy would have required a great deal of advocacy, not least because so many Americans – if the conventional media are to be believed – just wanted Afghanistan destroyed. However, the US President is an extremely powerful leader and President Bush could have assumed such a role, if he'd wanted to. It would have required him to ask Americans if there were another way to behave, and so encourage creative thinking based on human rights norms.

I've raised this alternative grand strategy because so often people persist with a military solution on the basis that 'there is no alternative'. And so we continue to get what we've always got; the human race doesn't seem to move forward. My philosophy in life is to try to look at how we might use a bad event to create a better future. But this requires a greater degree of creativity than we currently see in politics. Instead, I fear human rights will be further undermined in the future, because of the increased police power that has been granted to government agencies. And people who fight fire with fire usually just end up with ashes.

September 11 presented the west with some opportunities for creative thinking. The new millennium could have begun with a new way of dealing with international conflict. But that opportunity was missed.

4

❓ Are humans warlike by nature?

History is full of war. But are humans warlike by their very nature and so destined to keep fighting forever? Or is the appetite for war something we've learned and so could eventually unlearn?

The United Nations Educational, Scientific and Cultural Organization (UNESCO) is carrying out an important research project on this very question. In 1986, an international meeting of scientists was convened in Seville by the Spanish National Commission for UNESCO. It adopted a 'Statement on Violence' refuting the notion that organised human violence is biologically determined. In other words, humans are not genetically programmed to be violent towards each other.

This statement is now known as the Seville Statement.

Its core contains five propositions, which set out what *doesn't* cause war:

1. We humans haven't acquired war from our animal ancestors. Animals do not kill each other, as humans do, in a systematic way. Animals kill to eat. 'Fighting' is usually a highly ritualised activity between males seeking to gain the favours of females, and losers are not killed because they admit defeat by leaving the area.
2. We haven't inherited war from our forebears. Some societies have no tradition of warfare at all – such as the Inuit in Canada. Other societies have changed over time. For example, a thousand years ago the Vikings were the 'Khmer Rouge' of Western Europe; now Sweden produces Volvos and models.
3. War is not necessary to ensure a better standard of living. Humans can gain more from cooperation. For example, in the first fifty years of the nuclear era, the US spent AU$5.6 trillion (5.6 million million) on the nuclear arms race, which is more than the value of outstanding mortgage loans on every building in the US and could easily refund the reconstruction of every school in the US. It's clear that the US could easily have achieved a great deal by not devoting so much money to the arms race.
4. War is not a product of the biological composition of the brain. Humans need to be trained for war, and the pacifist tradition suggests that some humans find such training contrary to their own inclinations. The fact that warfare has changed so radically over time indicates that it is a product of culture. Human biology makes warfare possible but not inevitable.
5. War is not caused by some basic 'instinct' or any other single motivation. Modern war involves the institutional

use of personal characteristics such as obedience, suggestibility and idealism; social skills such as language; and rational considerations such as cost calculations, planning and information processing.

The Seville Statement concludes: 'Biology does not condemn humanity to violence and war. Instead, it is possible to end war and the suffering it causes. To do this will require everyone working together, but it must begin in the mind of each person with the belief that it is possible. The same human being who has made war is capable of constructing peace. Each of us has a task to do.'

UNESCO is now gaining international endorsement of the Seville Statement. Educational associations and other organisations are being invited to join the list of bodies that have already endorsed the Statement, and to distribute and publicise it. The Statement is beginning to be printed in textbooks and is being used in school and university lectures. Education is a slow process, but it is a thorough way of changing attitudes. By contrast, a glib advertising campaign would be just a fad, unlikely to last any longer than other advertised products.

There is a precedent for this kind of deep-seated educational campaign. At the end of World War II, UNESCO produced a statement on race that challenged the then fashionable notion that white people were somehow genetically superior to black people. That statement, through international endorsement and publicity, helped reshape attitudes to race. People may still be racist, but there are no respected scientific arguments to support their opinions.

The intention is to build a similar momentum in favour of the Seville Statement. People may continue to say that war is inevitable because it is somehow part of human nature, but they will not have the scientific arguments to support their opinions.

5

? What is the risk of a World War III?

The good news is that there is currently very little risk of a deliberate World War III. World Wars, by definition, require extensive political coalitions and military forces encircling the globe. The fear of World War III arose during the Cold War after 1945, which saw two military alliances, headed respectively by the United States and the Soviet Union, in a stand-off situation. The US and its allies and the Soviet Union and its allies were armed against each other in the largest military confrontation in world history. There were some close calls, such as the 1962 Cuban Missile Crisis, in which the US opposed the Soviet Union's installation of nuclear missiles on Cuba. For almost half a century, the Cold War was the central defining global political event. Most national governments made foreign policy decisions in the context of how it would affect their relationship with the US, or the Soviet Union, and help the US's, or Soviet Union's, overall Cold War aims.

The Cold War ended in the late 1980s with the disappearance of the Soviet Union, and deprived the US and its allies of their central foreign policy theme. The post-Cold War world is an uncertain place. The US spent forty-five years (1945–90) worrying about the power of Moscow and its potential threat to the rest of the world. Now it's worried that Moscow doesn't have enough power to maintain order within its own country, such as in combating Russia's organised crime.

The US had plans for war but not for peace. Since the Soviet Union has collapsed, many of its allies are seeking to join the military and economic alliances of the west, and Russia is trying to align itself with the US in the US's War on Terrorism.

The US and Russia both still have extensive nuclear weapons but they are no longer targeted at each other. There remains a risk of accidental nuclear warfare, or that a terrorist group could get control of the nuclear weapons, but this would not represent a world war as such.

The bad news is that while there's little fear of a World War III, there's also little hope of world peace. We've seen the rise of a new warfare state, where fighting is often internal rather than international and guerrilla rather than conventional. This means that much of the money countries devote to conventional military expenditure is wasted. Governments would be better off finding out why guerrilla groups resort to violence in the first place and trying to address the underlying economic and social causes of the violence.

To understand how the new warfare state has evolved, we need to look at the history of warfare and the scope for guerrilla warfare in the future.

First wave warfare: guerrilla

The oldest form of fighting is guerrilla warfare. It required little training, had no formal uniforms and used unsophisticated weapons based on everyday implements, usually farming tools. Guerrillas usually fought in a part-time capacity, in small bands who knew each other, which could comprise men, women and children.

The Roman army was the exception. Rather than adopt guerrilla tactics, it had professional soldiers with distinctive uniforms and fought in large, organised formations. In retrospect, it was a pioneer of modern warfare. However, it was not always successful in its campaigns against guerrilla forces.

During the thousand years or so of the European Middle Ages, no one paid much attention to the Roman military model. The wars of that era were mainly small battles by modern standards or sieges of fortified positions, such as castles. There were few full-time soldiers. Knights ran feudal estates as their main source of income, and recruited their own workers as troops when required.

Second wave warfare: conventional

Warfare changed around the seventeenth century. There isn't any single explanation for the change; it was more a matter of different events influencing each other. With the beginnings of the nation-state system, which international lawyers date from 1648, the basic unit of governance shifted from a small tribal area to the larger nation-state. This gave rulers more people from whom they could draw taxation and conscripts. The Industrial Revolution enabled the development of more destructive weapons and meant fighting formations could be transported over greater distances. Europeans could now fight each other over colonies in the Americas, Africa and Asia.

This new form of warfare became so common that it was called 'conventional' warfare. Fighting formations were larger, and almost exclusively male, so troops needed distinctive uniforms to distinguish them from the enemy. Armies also became more specialised in their work, defending national security rather than generally maintaining law and order. The latter task was given to a separate force: the police.

Armies and navies became more professional. Defence personnel were set apart from the rest of the community: they lived in separate buildings and were controlled by legal codes that were usually more extensive than those of the civilian legal system. Civilians' access to weapons was restricted and warfare became the exclusive right of the government. For the first time, there were professional soldiers who spent large chunks of time not fighting. Previously soldiers had been recruited for specific campaigns and demobilised as soon as the fighting stopped; now they had permanent employment but fighting only consumed part of their time.

During the first half of the twentieth century, the nature of conventional warfare changed. In World War I land warfare became far more mechanised. The last Allied cavalry charge was on 8 November 1917, when units of the Canadian army defeated a German cavalry regiment. By the time of World War II, there were few horses used in battle. In 1941, the UK had 100,000 vehicles in the Middle East. By the time of D-day in June 1944, there was one vehicle for every 4.77 Allied soldiers. From 1939–45, 130,000 aircraft were produced in the UK, 119,000 in Germany and 303,000 in the US. Warfare had become an activity of quartermasters and production planners.

The 'tail' became bigger than the 'teeth'. In order to keep one soldier at the front (the 'teeth'), there were six persons at the tail drawn from such civilian occupations as catering, engineering, medicine, building, transportation and law. Each arm of service became a society within a society.

World War II will always remain the world's largest conventional war. Other wars have been longer – notably the Iran–Iraq war of the 1980s – but none will ever be as extensive, intensive and expensive.

The cost of the mechanisation is the prime factor in the decline of conventional warfare. Humans were comparatively cheap – they often came via conscription – but machines are expensive to purchase and to maintain. The new B2 bomber, at $2.2 billion each, is said to cost three times its weight in gold.

The machines today are much more destructive as they can travel further with more firepower than previous weapons. But this also means they can be destroyed at a faster rate, with less chance of ever being repaired. Since the early 1960s, all major conventional wars, which have resulted in a clear victory, have been won in less than six weeks. If one side cannot defeat the other in that time, the war will just drag on, such as the inconclusive Iran–Iraq war, which ran for eight years. That crucial six-week period is based on the limitations of equipment and supply: governments can no longer afford to maintain large reserves of equipment.

Third wave warfare: nuclear weapons

Nuclear warfare was a direct outgrowth from conventional air warfare. Leaders in World War II wanted to avoid a repeat of World War I's trench warfare and so they looked for methods of moving firepower quickly over long distances.

Bomber aircraft were the favourite method throughout Europe. The technology of that period seems quaint by our standards half a century later. One of the RAF's most famous raids was in May 1943, when the 617 Squadron attacked some German dams. Scientist Barnes Wallis devised a bomb that would bounce along the length of the lake behind the dam and then hit the dam itself. The bomb had to be dropped from a height of precisely 18 metres, flying at 370 km/h. The bomb-aiming system was based on a coat-hanger: when the two nails on the hand-held sight lined up with the towers on the dam, the bomb had to be dropped. The raid was largely successful in destroying the dams and was a good boost for British morale, but only eleven of the nineteen aircraft returned home.

The quest continued for much more powerful bombs, and culminated in the creation of the atomic bomb. The atomic bomb brought the war against Japan to an abrupt end in August 1945 and so politicians reasoned that atomic weapons would be crucial in any future conflict. Later research shifted the emphasis from bombs transported by aircraft to missiles.

On a rate based on the number of potential deaths, nuclear missiles are cheaper than most other forms of killing. Ironically, their limitation arises from their extensive capacity to kill: they are too destructive to use in the usual military campaigns. Nuclear weapons would destroy everything the attacker hoped to win over and control.

Nuclear missiles cannot be shot down, which means, for the first time in history, that even the most powerful nation is unable to defend its people from an attack. Even if the US's proposed Strategic Defence Initiative ('star wars') had gone ahead and it could have shot down some missiles, it would only have taken about 2 per cent of Soviet missiles to destroy the US's main cities. I think President Bush's revised version of the program will be no more successful. The September 11 terrorists didn't use nuclear weapons to attack the US: they were in the country legally, they boarded four passenger aircraft legally and then used the aircraft with their heavy supplies of aviation fuel as their weapons.

The 1987 US–USSR agreement on intermediate nuclear forces and the 1993 US–Russia agreement on strategic nuclear weapons showed that both countries realised the limitations of these weapons for political purposes. But the US remains vulnerable to nuclear attack because of the number of Russian strategic missiles still in existence. The US was actually much safer from attack in 1945 than it now is. Back in 1945, there were no missiles or bombers that could fly from Europe to reach the US. The US mainland was a very safe country from foreign attack because it was so distant from all the international trouble spots. Apart from a random Japanese submarine attack on California in the early years of World War II, there was no foreign attack on the US mainland between 1812 (the war with Britain) and 11 September 2001. No other continent enjoyed such haven from international violence.

Unfortunately all societies remain vulnerable to guerrilla groups using nuclear explosive devices. The nuclear weapon cannot be un-invented; that knowledge is here to stay.

Fourth wave warfare: the return of guerrilla warfare

Most wars under way today are not strictly 'international' – that is, one nation attacking another, or groups of nations attacking each other, using conventional warfare. The modern trends in warfare are for groups to try to break away from an existing nation to create their own nation, or for a group to try to overthrow its government and so form its own government. Guerrilla warfare is the preferred technique in both cases.

Guerrilla warfare has grown rapidly since World War II. Almost every war under way today involves guerrillas in at least one party to the conflict. As in the earlier guerrilla era, they fight in small bands and often don't have a uniform. The difference is that these days they are often fighting with very sophisticated weapons, either donated by more powerful countries or stolen from the enemy's conventional forces. And while there is now virtually no risk of a World War III, there is a growing risk that guerrilla groups will eventually get access to nuclear weapons. The weapons need not be very sophisticated and the 'delivery system' could be the back of a truck.

Guerrilla warfare turns conventional warfare's reasoning upside down. It's not so much about taking and holding a set piece of territory as about winning the hearts and minds of people; it's essentially political. Guerrilla warfare is also a form of attrition, a wearing down of the conventional forces until exhaustion and frustration set in. Guerrillas can lose battle after battle and yet still win the war. Furthermore, guerrillas don't need a large amount of firepower since they are only carrying out sporadic raids. In fact, too much firepower can alienate the local population – as US troops discovered in Vietnam – since there is a temptation to use it wantonly. It could be argued that the US didn't lose in Vietnam because of a shortage of firepower, but partly because of their excessive use of it.

Modern life in large cities is anonymous and next-door neighbours often know little about each other. A guerrilla group could operate from a city district and not even the people living close by would know. This anonymity makes it difficult for the police to get information. Guerrillas can disappear in the crowd, like fish in a sea.

And as modern life has become more sophisticated, so it has become more vulnerable to disruption. For example, a century or so ago Australian homes had to look after their own water supply, and so each household was far more self-reliant than it is today with its dependence on a centralised reticulation system. Electricity is now also centrally supplied. A guerrilla group wouldn't have been able to disrupt a town's water or electricity supply a century ago, but that's not the case nowadays.

In 1965 and 1977, New York City and parts of the northeast US suffered electrical collapses. They were accidental but they revealed how vulnerable New York is to electrical disruptions. A guerrilla group with a knowledge of the grid system could put the city out of action for much longer.

Modern transport is also of great use to guerrillas, giving them greater mobility. For example, a group may attack the offices of its opponent (its embassy) in another nation. Modern transport also provides targets – particularly airports and aircraft – where security is difficult to maintain, and so a dispute in one nation can easily spill over into other nations.

A further implication of the growth of guerrilla warfare is that civilians now bear the brunt of the fighting. One of the key factors of conventional warfare was the clear distinction between professional soldiers and civilians: one protected the other and, in return, received a special status in society. Senior officers have a senior standing at official government functions in recognition of their willingness to lay down their lives to protect the rest of society. Male members of royal families traditionally serve for a few years in the defence forces.

However, from World War II onwards, the percentage of civilians being killed in warfare has increased. This is to be expected given the changed nature of warfare: once, military personnel and buildings were the exclusive targets. These days, the targets could be anything – including office blocks. Civilian deaths may now be as high as 90 per cent of the total deaths in warfare.

We can see, then, that guerrillas operate in a different way from conventional forces. Using conventional forces against a guerrilla army is like fighting lung cancer while continuing to smoke cigarettes: it's a futile exercise if no attention is given to the cause – in this case, the smoking itself. But conventional forces are trained for military action, not to analyse why people go to war in the first place; and politicians prefer what they see as 'quick solutions' and so tend to use force rather than seek the underlying causes of conflict. A more conciliatory approach to Tamil grievances some years ago, for example, could have reduced the subsequent Sri Lankan and Indian bloodshed.

The USSR's operation in Afghanistan showed that it didn't understand the unique nature of guerrilla warfare and that it hadn't learnt a thing from the US's experience in Vietnam. Much the same could be said about the Israelis in the Occupied Territories or the Burmese forces in Karen-controlled eastern Burma.

The mass media's contribution to guerrilla warfare

Although comparatively few people are killed in guerrilla raids, the deaths attract a disproportionate amount of news coverage. For example, more people are killed on the roads of Northern Ireland each year than are killed in the warfare there. But wars sell newspapers. The mass media are effectively publicising guerrilla attacks.

In 1985, the then British prime minister, Margaret Thatcher, called for the media to show greater restraint in reporting guerrilla activities. She said that we had to try to find ways to starve the terrorist and the hijacker of the oxygen of publicity they depend on. In democratic societies we don't believe in constraining the media or in censorship, but is it unreasonable to ask the media to agree among themselves on a voluntary code of conduct under which they would not print or broadcast anything that might assist the terrorists' morale or their cause during the time of the hijack or other terrorist activity? Nothing came of Mrs Thatcher's suggestion. Only in wartime can a government try to censor the media, and although the IRA problem was serious it certainly did not amount to a 'war'. Mrs Thatcher could not therefore try to acquire any power of strict censorship.

Mrs Thatcher's idea of self-restraint wasn't such an unusual one. For example, the mass media are very careful about how they report suicides of 'ordinary people' – not only out of respect for the next of kin but also to avoid 'copy-cat' deaths. (By contrast, the rich and famous get as much coverage in death as in life.)

When it comes to deaths caused by guerrilla warfare, however, the media continue to report on them extensively, and guerrilla groups seem to grow even more adept at using the media to convey their point of view.

AQ Khan and the nuclear black market

Dr Abdul Qadeer ('AQ') Khan, a national hero in Pakistan, is known as the father of the 'Islamic bomb'. He is also known to have contributed to creating an international black market for the supply of nuclear material.

An Islamic–Communist alliance between Pakistan and China arose from their mutual concerns over India, after

India acquired its own nuclear weapons in readiness for its twenty-first-century superpower status, when it will eventually rival China. India has few military worries about Pakistan, which it could beat easily without nuclear weapons. But China is a different matter.

China helped Pakistan build its own nuclear weapons to put pressure on India. This wasn't such a wise move because China now has a crisis on its hands. The scientist China aided in the building of the bomb, AQ Khan, has secretly sold material to North Korea. Clearly, he's not just a smart scientist; he's a smart businessperson as well. Now China is having to lead the international initiative to restrain North Korea's nuclear ambitions. China wants to attract foreign investment, but who is willing to risk investment in a country that borders the erratic, nuclear-armed North Korean regime?

The AQ Khan saga gets worse. We know that he sold nuclear material to Libya too. Libya is now coming in from the cold and wants to improve its links with the west, so it has come clean about its own nuclear ambitions. But who else has had dealings with AQ Khan? The CIA would like to know, but the Pakistani Government won't allow their national hero to be interrogated by the Americans.

Here's a nightmare scenario. AQ Khan may also have sold nuclear material to terrorists associated with Osama bin Laden. These terrorists could use it in a nuclear attack on the US. If that does happen, Americans will be enraged that the US Government knew about AQ Khan's black market activities, yet did nothing to remove him from Pakistan and interrogate him.

6

❓ Should Third World debt be forgiven?

Yes, Third World debt should be forgiven because in most cases the original debt has been repaid. Now it's more a matter of paying interest on the interest. Poor developing countries owe developed countries – such as Australia – about US$500 billion. Every day they repay about US$100 million to rich western countries, which means they spend more money in debt repayment than they receive in foreign aid. This is one of the biggest international scandals in recent decades.

In June 2005, finance ministers of the Group of Eight (G8), the world's richest countries, agreed to drop some of the debt – about 10 per cent. This is a move in the right direction, but there is a lot more to be done.

How did the debt get created?

When the European colonies were wound up, starting in the 1950s, the new countries needed money to finance some of their development projects.

A major source of money after 1973 came from the Arab 'petro-dollars'. In 1973, the Arab countries in the Organization of Petroleum Exporting Countries (OPEC) dramatically increased the price of oil during the 1973 Middle East War. Western countries couldn't operate without the oil and so they had to pay the much higher prices. The revenue (in US dollars) poured into the Arab countries.

The money had to be recycled through the international finance system or else it would just accumulate in the Arab countries. Those Arab countries spent (and often wasted) a lot of money on themselves, but there was still some left over and, as Muslims, they felt it should be made available to poorer people. Developing countries borrowed some of that money.

In the 1980s, due to President Reagan's expansion of the arms race against the Soviet Union, the US Government started to get into debt itself and so had to borrow money on the international market. Global interest rates went up and developing countries often found themselves unable to repay the money they'd borrowed.

No developing country government has actually defaulted on any loan. If a government were to do so, it wouldn't be able to borrow again. So how does a government raise the money to repay the debt? It can't take it from the police or the military, as either service could rebel and remove a government. Instead, the money comes from welfare and education expenditure.

The UN estimates that 7 million children die unnecessarily each year from diseases that can be cured and from unclean water that could be made safe. If the money poor countries pay to richer countries in debt service were spent instead on tackling poverty, the lives of millions of children in poor countries would be saved.

The debt crisis has lingered on the international agenda for about two decades. Some non-government organisations, such as the Christian-backed Jubilee 2000, and some musical entertainers have taken up the cause. But it hasn't been a major issue for most western politicians.

Why not forgive the entire debt?

Opponents of forgiving the debt argue that to do so would be a 'moral hazard'. In other words, once a government was excused the debt on one occasion, it would be tempted to get into debt again in the expectation that this debt would also be forgiven in due course.

Some of this concern can be countered by ensuring there are mechanisms in place to monitor how the government spends its money in future. For example, Uganda first got debt relief in 1998, when almost a fifth of its national budget was taken up by debt repayments. The government agreed that the money that would previously have gone in debt repayments would in future be spent on the country's health and education systems.

Personally, I am wary of international financiers lecturing others on morality. Their hands aren't always clean. Many haven't just lent money to corrupt dictators; they've also handled their funds. Let's take the Philippines as an example. Three decades ago, the corrupt Marcos Government ordered a nuclear reactor from an American company. The reactor was built on an earthquake fault near Manila and so will never produce electricity. Coincidentally, I was on the election platform with presidential candidate Mrs Aquino in January 1986 when she promised that, if she beat President Marcos in the presidential election, she wouldn't go ahead with completing the reactor. She won the election and she kept her promise. But her government – and her successors – still had to pay the debt on that useless reactor: about US$250,000 per day. The final cost of the reactor was three times the original estimate, and the difference was invested by President Marcos in foreign real estate. The international financiers knew exactly what they were doing when they handled that money.

Other solutions to Third World debt

The June 2005 initiative is a good start, but there's still the other 90 per cent to forgive. At the current rate of progress, it will be decades before that happens.

For almost forty years governments have been asked to give 0.7 per cent of their gross national product (GNP) each year as foreign aid. They shouldn't now include any debt forgiveness as part of that 0.7 per cent. Debt cancellation is a matter of justice not foreign aid.

The few debt-forgiveness schemes that have been introduced so far have often included demands that the developing countries privatise their health and education schemes. What developing countries really need are schemes without any harmful strings attached. The World Bank and International Monetary Fund (IMF), both of which were originally created to help development, are now heavily focused on debt repayment. They prefer to keep governments as far removed as possible from running national economies and leave the economy to the 'market'. The problem is, the market is good for economic growth but not necessarily for distributing wealth.

What we need to see is the creation of a new, international, fair, transparent and comprehensive process to resolve the debt crisis. For example, such a system could decide on whether 'odious debts' incurred by dictators (such as Marcos in the Philippines and Suharto in Indonesia) should still be repaid. At the moment, decisions like this are made behind the closed doors of the World Bank and IMF, and, because these institutions have voting systems based on economic wealth, the US dominates them in the 'weighted voting' – that is, each country has a different number of votes based on the size of its economy. The richer the country, the more votes it has.

Finally, to avoid a recurrence of the debt crisis, all future monies to developing countries should be given as grants and not loans. However, even if all Third World debt was forgiven, there are still many other barriers to development (see 'Is foreign aid a waste of money?').

The Bretton Woods System

The world is richer now than ever before. Some of the foundations for this wealth were laid in 1944 at a luxury hotel in the United States. The US hosted an international conference at Bretton Woods, New Hampshire, to create a new international economic order that would have the US at its centre.

This new order was based on the US dollar – rather than the British pound – and it created two international financial institutions: the World Bank and the International Monetary Fund (IMF), both based in Washington DC near the White House. The World Bank provides long-term development loans and the IMF helps governments with short-term loans during economic crises.

The new system meant the end of British economic dominance. The old international economic order had been run from London. In the seventeenth and eighteenth centuries, British traders went in search of markets and did deals with local rulers. Later on, in the nineteenth century, British influence was solidified by direct British rule and a formal empire was created. The British 'tribe' dwelling around the globe provided what was then the world's best financial network.

Meanwhile, the US developed quickly in the late nineteenth and early twentieth centuries behind a wall of tariffs and other protective measures. By 1939, the US produced about a third of the world's manufactures, which was more than twice the production of Nazi Germany and almost ten times that of Japan.

By the late 1930s, US companies were interested in foreign markets, but many of these lay behind the wall of British 'imperial preferences'. The British empire was based on sterling – the world's main currency at the time – and British investment and colonial exports were all prioritised within the empire. If the US wanted to challenge British dominance, it had to remove that system of imperial preferences.

Meanwhile, World War II went on longer than expected and the US became worried that the long-term financial result would be a post-war world consisting of bankrupt countries heavily in debt to the US. That would put the US in the prime financial position, but there was little hope for continued US expansion if there were no foreign markets for US goods. There was also the risk that bankrupt countries would be unstable and so face fresh threats from Nazi or Communist movements and governments.

The international economy had to be rebuilt and this would be best achieved with the US at the financial centre. In 1945, the US commanded 40 per cent of the world's economy. It wanted the US dollar to become the basic international currency, with countries committed to free trade, thereby ending the system of imperial preferences.

The Bretton Woods System – which Australia had an active role in creating – formed part of the basis for a golden period of economic growth in the 1950s and removed the fear of another 1930s-style Depression.

The Bretton Woods conference was one of the most productive conferences held last century. But now there are demands for a better system, more reflective of the interests of developing countries, which didn't exist in 1944.

7

❓ What is the McDonald's Golden Arches Theory of World Peace?

This is the argument that countries that sell McDonald's fast food do not go to war against each other. There's nothing special about fast food reducing a person's ability to fight; it's simply that countries that accept fast-food outlets are embracing free trade, and free trade reduces the risk of war.

Trade and transnational corporations are knitting the world together. For over a thousand years, the Franks and Huns – now the French and Germans – fought one another. Now they've gone for a generation without a war and it seems unlikely they'll ever have another one. Why would they kill off their customers?

There are probably as many conflicts under way today as there were at the height of the Cold War, but these days they are increasingly internal rather than international.

The decline of international conflict has been credited partly to the growth of free trade and democracy. Governments are now committed to free trade and free politics, and capitalism creates a thriving middle class. Middle-class people are more globally oriented. They spin webs of affiliation around the world. They create non-governmental organisations (NGOs) such as Amnesty International and Greenpeace, as well as transnational corporations. War is bad for their interests. Middle-class people prefer a world where they can travel freely – both to make money and to satisfy their curiosity – and are less tolerant of prolonged wars. Mrs Thatcher could unite the British in 1982 for the short, sharp Falklands campaign of six weeks, but President Johnson couldn't unite the US for the five years of his Vietnam campaign.

Invasions used to be about the conquest of new territory and resources or the imposition of a religion upon new converts. These days, little is to be gained by one country invading another. In the new era of information technology, much of a country's wealth is in the heads of its people or in cyberspace. What would a country get from invading Japan, say? Japan has few natural resources. By the same token, Iraq's invasion of Kuwait in August 1990 was a bad investment because so much of Kuwait's financial reserves were held offshore.

Of course, old rivalries will remain and there are traditional border disputes. When a country has problems at home it is always tempting to focus attention on an external threat; take Greece and Turkey, for example, or India and Pakistan. But there are few international wars under way at present. Governments are finding that they have more to gain from peace than from war. Even the Indians and Pakistanis, for all their posturing with nuclear weapons, seem reluctant to enter deliberately into another war.

Global trade

Such changes are the result of global trade. Global business has changed the pattern of economic relationships. For example, before the Industrial Revolution in the eighteenth century, when most English people were peasant farmers living in villages, their village institutions were dominated by the values of localism and self-sufficiency. What little trade there was took place between people who knew each other. That pattern of life has gone. In Australia today, a trip to the supermarket to buy food for the weekend is in itself an experience in global trade, though the consumer would probably be unaware of it. There is little that is locally (ie Australian) made. Music, movies, telephones, clothes, cars, petrol, for example, often come from overseas.

National governments no longer have full control over their economies. Take the inability of governments to generate full employment, for example. We're currently seeing the transfer of some kinds of jobs from developed to developing countries, where labour costs are low or where there isn't a shortage of specialist workers. Bangalore in India has been dubbed the 'Silicon Plateau' – to rival California's Silicon Valley – as more than thirty companies, including Motorola, IBM, Texas Instruments, Hewlett Packard and Citicorp, have set up software-programming offices there.

Many of the jobs lost in developed countries will never return. The manufacturing industry is going the way of agriculture: few people work on the land these days, but those that do are more productive than ever before thanks to the assistance of machines. Much the same could be said for factories in developed countries: the workers that remain will be more productive than ever before due to improvements in mechanisation.

Transnational corporations encourage the intertwining of national economies; they themselves move across national boundaries and so forge links between countries. But this intertwining limits the scope of government action. These corporations don't need a host government to open up or guarantee foreign markets; they can do better on their own. In fact, national identification can be a burden. If a product is identified with a particular country – such as Coca-Cola and the US – then a government may try to keep that product out simply to show its displeasure with US foreign policy. It's notable that the few countries where Coke isn't sold are those that are antagonistic to the US, such as North Korea.

Global consumers

Consumerism is the leading edge of the globalised economy and has resulted in the creation of a global middle class. The global middle class often have more in common with members of the middle class in other countries than they do with the working class or poor within their own country. For example, a US-based corporation will be more concerned with selling to the emerging middle class in India or other parts of Asia, than to the people in the US who can't afford to buy its products. So Coke is the global soft drink, McDonald's is the global fast food and CNN is the global television network. These are the commodities of a new global middle class.

The US made a major mistake in the mid-1940s, during the Cold War, when implementing its policy of 'containment'. The US and its allies encircled the Soviet Union and its Eastern European allies with a network of military alliances to stop any potential expansion. The US saw the 'Soviet threat' as essentially a military one to be opposed on military lines. Therefore the US opposed the Soviet Union on the Soviet Union's own grounds rather than its own. It failed to understand that a centrally planned economy can make military weapons but has much greater difficulty making consumer goods. A government committee of old men living a comparatively luxurious and isolated existence in Moscow has no real idea of the ordinary person's consumer tastes. The USSR was able to keep in the arms race (although the US overestimated the Soviet Union's strength) but it couldn't match the US's production of consumer goods. The Soviet Union could put people into space but it couldn't put consumer goods on shop shelves.

Few predicted the collapse of the Soviet Union from within. Western Cold War politicians saw the arms race as the key component of the Cold War but ignored the everyday basics. Soviet citizens were yearning for the 'good things of life' and recognised that the Soviet system couldn't produce Coke, Big Macs and Madonna. They may have been militarily loyal to Moscow, but their hearts were in the US – after all, Hollywood makes the best dreams. And while President Reagan in the early 1980s regarded the USSR as the 'evil empire', transnational corporations saw Soviet citizens as potential customers.

Alexander Solzhenitsyn, arguably Russia's greatest writer of the twentieth century, provides an example of the impact of consumer culture. Solzhenitsyn saw himself as a 'conscience' during the Communist era and was a critic of the regime. He was eventually expelled from the Soviet Union in 1974 and lived in exile in Vermont in the US. In 1989, with the Soviet regime in trouble, Solzhenitsyn insisted that his books had to be available in book stores in the USSR before he would return. In 1994, he went home for the first time in two decades. The Soviet regime had gone and his books were in the shops, but few copies were being sold. Instead, consumers were buying the kinds of books available in the west: on sport, sex, romance and entertainment. They didn't want to read about the suffering under Communism; they wanted escape from it.

The impact of television has also played a major role in the development of a global consumer culture. Television advertising ensures that Coca-Cola is the global soft drink and Big Macs are the global fast food. The grass-roots NGOs in Eastern Europe, which campaigned for an end to the Cold War and free movement of people throughout the continent, were partly motivated by the desire to gain access to the 'good things' in western life. Revolutions go better with Coke.

Global consumerism in India

Mahatma Gandhi hoped his country would become economically self-sufficient. He stopped wearing foreign shirts and wore a *khaddar* made with home-spun cotton as a political trademark. This set an example for others and became the symbol of India's campaign for freedom. But many Indians are now active participants in the global economy.

Since the early 1990s, foreign shirts have increased in popularity and are being made in India under licence from transnational corporations. Satellite television reaches about 600 million people (out of a total of about 1 billion) and appeals particularly to the emerging middle class, which is growing at about 20 million per year. Unlike China, India has imposed few restrictions on television advertising and so this fuels the demand for consumer goods.

The problem is that expectations are rising faster than the capacity of any Indian government to satisfy them. It seems hard to believe that the Indian standard of living could ever reach US levels, but politicians are obliged to keep assuring voters that living standards are going to get better. If they don't make that promise, other candidates will certainly do so – and get elected. For the emerging middle class these promises may be true, but many people will never enter that class. Additionally, there will be environmental limits to India's growth – as is the case with the economic growth of all countries – and the Indian nation-state is likely to suffer huge environmental strains in the future.

8

❓ Should New Zealand merge with Australia?

New Zealand was offered the opportunity to merge with Australia a century ago but turned it down. The two countries have maintained a strongly separate identity since British colonisation.

In 1769–70, Britain's James Cook sailed the South Pacific looking for a 'Great South Land'. For centuries Europeans had assumed there must be a giant landmass in the south to balance the Europe/Asia landmass in the north. Cook reported back that there was no giant landmass, just a variety of different-sized islands in a huge expanse of water.

The British set about colonising New South Wales and New Zealand. They started with New South Wales, because Cook had reported that the local people were more pleasant: they were inoffensive and not given to cruelty. The few Maori

Cook saw scared him, and on his second voyage in 1774, ten of his crew members were killed and eaten by Maori.

New South Wales was set up as a British penal colony. Of the 30,000 prisoners sent to Sydney, Hobart or Norfolk Island, about 3000 managed to escape, making a dash for New Zealand. New Zealanders are proud that, other than these 'boat people', they never received any convicts. New Zealand's European heritage came from settlers who moved to the country of their own free will. Early migration schemes boasted that New Zealand was 'another England' – a green and pleasant land suitable for farming – while Australia was parched and snake-ridden.

British visitors to both Australia and New Zealand often note the different cultures. Some say that Australians have a relaxed 'she'll do, mate' mentality, possibly partly reflective of the country's Irish Catholic working-class or convict origins, while New Zealanders, who were settled by tough Scottish Presbyterians, take themselves more seriously. Others seem to take New Zealand seriously as well. New Zealand is a country of only 4 million people yet, in recent years, it has produced the Secretary General of the World Trade Organization (WTO) in Geneva and the Secretary General of the Commonwealth Secretariat in London.

By the time of the emerging Commonwealth of Australia in the nineteenth century, New Zealanders had developed a strong national identity and didn't want to merge with Australia. To people outside the region, the people of both countries looked similar. But the people themselves felt different; they had no common sense of identity. So when Australians campaigning for the 1901 national federation gave New Zealanders the opportunity to be represented at their constitutional conferences, the New Zealanders replied that transport across the Tasman was inadequate and they knew as little about Australia as they did about Africa. They also feared they didn't have the money to keep political representatives based in Australia for months on end. Meanwhile, there was a movement within New Zealand emphasising the need to remain separate from Australia.

The Australian Constitution retains a provision that enables New Zealand to join the federation if it wants to, but New Zealand shows very little formal political interest in doing so. And in this new era of globalisation, there's really no need for the countries to merge. Finance and people can move easily across the two countries' national borders, and some New Zealanders have made their own decisions about joining Australia.

Over one-tenth of all New Zealanders (450,000) now live in Australia. In fact, there are many more New Zealanders living in Australia than there are Australian Indigenous peoples. The average New Zealander living in Australia enjoys a higher standard of living than the average Australian and is better educated and better paid. In contrast, only about 60,000 Australians live in New Zealand.

9

? Why did the United States invade Iraq?

There is no single explanation for the US's invasion of Iraq. Instead, here are eight hypotheses. I'm not fully convinced about any one of them, although the eighth – and most sinister – seems to have lasted the course better than the others.

As a response to 11 September 2001

The terrorist attacks on September 11 marked the first time the US had been attacked on its mainland since the war against the British in 1812. Many Americans believed that Saddam Hussein was responsible for the attacks. During my television commentaries on the 2003 campaign, I noticed the many young American military personnel who said they were willing to attack Iraq to avenge the events of September 11. But there is no evidence at all that Saddam Hussein had any involvement in the September 11 attacks and he still denies it. There were no Iraqis among the hijackers. Iraq was not a terrorist threat to the US.

On 11 September 2002, I was in New York to comment on the anniversary events for September 11. It was one of the most moving days of my life. The following morning, President Bush addressed the United Nations General Assembly. We were surprised that most of his speech was devoted to dealing not with Osama bin Laden, but with Saddam Hussein.

Saddam Hussein and Osama bin Laden were not natural allies. Saddam Hussein was socialist (in the Stalin style) and nationalist, without any fundamentalist Islamic sympathy. Osama bin Laden is a fundamentalist Muslim who wants to recreate the traditional Caliphate religious leader who would rule right across the Arab world. This means Saddam Hussein would have been answerable to a higher Islamic authority – something he'd never have wanted.

It may even be that Osama bin Laden privately welcomed the US attack on Iraq in 2003. He didn't like Saddam Hussein's regime because it wasn't Islamic enough for him; and it was a possibility that the attack would drag the US into another military quagmire – which it has – and so weaken it. The attack also vindicated Osama bin Laden's criticisms of the US as an aggressive country and so might increase fundamentalist Islamic support for him, which is probably the case. It might also lead to the destabilisation of Saudi Arabia, whose ruling family bin Laden wants to overthrow. This hasn't yet happened, but the ruling family's life has not been made any easier by the war, which they didn't support. (They did support the US in the 1990–91 Gulf War with free oil.)

Ironically, there was only ever one link between Saddam Hussein and Osama bin Laden: in the 1980s both received aid from the US. Saddam Hussein received US military assistance when he launched a war against Iran, which was also a US enemy. The current Defence Secretary, Donald Rumsfeld, was President Ronald Reagan's emissary to Saddam Hussein. Meanwhile, in Afghanistan, Osama bin Laden was part of the Islamic resistance to the Soviet Union's invading force after 1979 and so received US military aid as part of the US's support of the Afghani resistance movement.

To wage a war against fundamentalist Islam

Clearly, the idea that the US went to war with Iraq as a way of countering fundamentalist Islam is not a good explanation, as Saddam Hussein's Iraq wasn't as fundamentalist as many of its Arab neighbours such as Saudi Arabia. Women in Iraq played a greater role in public life than did those in many of the neighbouring countries; and indeed one of the chief scientists of the weapons of mass destruction program was a woman. Saddam Hussein ran a secular regime during the 1980s and 1990s and was suspicious of Islamic fundamentalism. He, like all his predecessors, was from the minority Sunnis and so he was worried about the power of the majority Shi'as, many of whom were fundamentalist. Some of his worst violence was directed at these people. Fundamentalist Muslims internationally are not entirely sorry that Saddam Hussein was removed, but they are not necessarily grateful to the US for doing it. It was only after his 1990 invasion of Kuwait that his regime became a little more religious, when he hoped he might get some Islamic support to oppose the US.

Now that Saddam Hussein has gone, there is a risk that the more fundamentalist Shi'as, who were excluded from Iraqi power and persecuted under Saddam Hussein, may gain more influence. Iraq may become a more explicitly 'Islamic' country in the future than it was in the past.

To find weapons of mass destruction

Iraq had long had weapons of mass destruction, particularly chemical ones. There were even fears of nuclear ones, which prompted Israel to unilaterally bomb the French-built nuclear reactor in Iraq on 7 June 1981 to destroy that threat. But were there still chemical or biological or nuclear weapons in Iraq in 2002? On 12 September 2002, President Bush called on the UN to do more to force Iraq to get rid of its weapons of mass destruction (WMD): that is, any chemical and biological weapons and any nuclear weapons it may have.

After Iraq was driven out of Kuwait in 1991, it remained the subject of UN sanctions until it disposed of its WMD. Saddam Hussein played a cat-and-mouse game of cheat and retreat with the UN: he would allow its inspectors into Iraq, then find a way of expelling them; be forced by international pressure to readmit them, then find another excuse to expel them; and so on. By the end of the 1990s, the international community was sick of the dictator's games. Also, there was growing concern about the numbers of Iraqis who were dying because they were unable to receive foreign goods and services due to the UN sanctions.

Iraq certainly had WMD in the early 1990s. Saddam Hussein's campaign against the Kurdish minority in northern Iraq in the late 1980s was the largest use of chemical warfare since World War I. And the UN teams of weapons inspectors –

which included some Australian scientists – found WMD in Iraq in the early 1990s.

But did Iraq still have any WMD by the end of the 1990s? If such weapons had survived the 1990s intact, they would have deteriorated by the end of the decade as chemical and biological weapons go stale over a period of time and lose their fatal qualities. The research and manufacturing facilities were still there, however, and could have continued their deadly activities.

We now know that it's unlikely there were any WMD left by 2003, when the US invaded Iraq. Why, then, did Saddam Hussein carry on with the cheat-and-retreat game? Possibly it was a matter of 'face': he didn't want to admit that he'd given in to international pressure. Maybe he wanted to give the impression that he still had WMD in order to deter attack, either from the US or neighbouring countries such as Iran, against which he had fought one of the longest wars of the twentieth century. Possibly his own scientists and generals preferred to deceive the dictator rather than admit their failure to continue making the weapons. Thanks to the UN sanctions they would have had difficulty obtaining the necessary materials from overseas.

Saddam Hussein certainly didn't pose any threat to the US. Ironically, since the US invaded in 2003, over 1700 Americans have been killed in Iraq.

As a result of faulty intelligence

No one doubts now that President Bush, and British Prime Minister Tony Blair, received faulty intelligence. This fact has been reaffirmed by the 2004 Butler inquiry in the UK and the March 2004 report to the US President.

Iraqi 'watchers', both within the intelligence community and outside (such as myself), had perhaps got into an intellectual rut. It was hard to believe that Saddam Hussein had no WMD, having seen him use them against the Kurds in the late 1980s. Also, we knew that from the early 1990s Iran had had WMD and that Saddam would do anything he could to stockpile his own in retaliation. Personally, I was sceptical about the 2003 war, because I feared the US would be sucked into a quagmire, but I did believe that Iraq still had some WMD. Saddam Hussein had lied so often that I couldn't believe that he was now telling the truth.

But did all this suspicion justify a war? No. And few people – if any – are now supporting the role of the intelligence agencies.

The problem is that intelligence is a very inexact science. The James Bond movies have created the impression that intelligence agencies work with the efficiency of a Swiss watch. (In a similar way, 'CSI'-style television programs have created unrealistic expectations about what police forces can do to detect criminals.) In fact, there have been some atrocious intelligence failures, to which Iraq should now be added. To complicate matters further, by the time 'raw' intelligence works its way up the chain of command, there's a tendency for it to become coloured by the political persuasions of the politicians who will be its ultimate readers. The editors in the agencies know what their political masters want to read and tailor the message accordingly.

For example, we now know that during the Vietnam War, CIA field staff kept reporting that the war couldn't be won. But the closer their reports got to the White House, the more they were changed to create the 'spin' that the war was winnable.

There's clearly a need for greater honesty within the intelligence agencies. On the other hand, being honest could be a career-limiting move. Why tell the truth when you know your political masters have already decided to go to war?

To get access to oil

Iraq has the Middle East's second-largest oil reserves. Saudi Arabia has the largest reserves, but it's an unstable regime and so it makes sense to diversify the sources of supply. When the US troops entered Baghdad in 2003, one of their first missions was to protect the Oil Ministry from looters – at the cost of the protection of the priceless National Museum (which, incidentally, was well signposted).

But is Iraq's oil supply enough of a reason for the US 2003 attack? I doubt it. After all, Saddam Hussein was happy to sell his oil overseas when he could – before the UN imposed sanctions on Iraq after his 1990 invasion of Kuwait. All the US needed to do was find a way of ending the UN sanctions and Iraq would be selling them oil again.

President Bush's way of ending the UN sanctions was to invade Iraq, but this has made each barrel of oil – when mass production starts again – incredibly expensive. The production facilities in the Iraqi oil fields have become rundown because of the UN sanctions, and so getting the oil fields flowing again would be an expensive job. On top of this, having a war has only added to the theoretical cost of each barrel.

President Bush's prediction that the 2003 war would be a cheap one, because it would be over quickly and Iraq could pay for its own reconstruction from its oil revenue, has been proved wrong. There is money to be made from the oil, but not yet. The ongoing guerrilla war means that the oil fields are still dangerous places for the oil industry to operate, let alone all the other costs associated with drilling and transportation. It will be some years before Iraqi oil is again highly profitable.

Because Saddam Hussein was an evil dictator

Saddam Hussein had an appalling record of violence, both against his own people and against his neighbours, such as Iran and Kuwait. I have supported the cause of the Iraqi Kurds since the early 1970s, when I met some of their supporters in London, and so I am glad that Saddam Hussein is gone.

President Bush's problem, however, is that he sought 'regime change' in Iraq, which was not part of the UN sanctions program. The UN simply wanted an end to WMD production and deployment, and proof that Iraq was not going to attack its neighbours again. The UN, as a matter of policy, rarely gets into the business of seeking to change government leaders – although one exception was the campaign for the removal of Ian Smith's illegal white regime (1965–80) in Rhodesia/Zimbabwe.

The problem with seeking 'regime change' is: where do you draw the line? If you're going to remove Saddam Hussein, why not also put an end to North Korea's dictatorship or Zimbabwe's Robert Mugabe? How are we to decide when 'regime change' is necessary? What should be the criteria?

All governments follow a policy of selective indignation: there are some governments and leaders they ignore and some they oppose. Australia took a very weak line on East Timor from 1975 until the late 1990s because it didn't want to annoy

Indonesia, which invaded East Timor in 1975. Australia supported the Indonesian occupation and did a deal with Indonesia to divide up East Timor's seabed oil.

Similarly, the US held a basic sympathy for Saddam Hussein in the 1980s, following his attack on Iran. Saddam Hussein was a nasty person, but for the US the Iranian regime was even nastier. At some point, however, probably the August 1990 Iraqi invasion of Kuwait, the US decided that Saddam Hussein was now even more of a worry than Iran.

President Bush was completing his father's business

This is a variation of the previous explanation. Although the US-led force, authorised by President George Bush senior, drove Iraq out of Kuwait in early 1991, it didn't chase the Iraqi forces over the border into Baghdad and destroy Saddam Hussein's regime. The US had no UN mandate for such an operation; the mandate was simply to liberate Kuwait. To have destroyed Saddam Hussein's regime at this time might also have shattered the coalition: the Arab nation-states were happy to see Kuwait liberated, but they didn't like the idea of the US occupying another Arab country.

President Bush senior (1988–92) and then President Clinton (1992–2000) had a sophisticated policy of keeping Saddam Hussein down but not out. They couldn't destroy him, because there was no obvious replacement for him (as we have seen for ourselves since the January 2005 election in Iraq). There was no Nelson Mandela-type figure waiting in the wings to take over, as happened with the fall of the white racist regime in South Africa. Saddam Hussein had long ago killed off all potential successors. And the US couldn't destroy Iraq itself – setting aside the international law implications of that – because a wrecked Iraq would create a power vacuum to be filled by either Iran or Syria, neither of which was pro-US and would result in an anti-US regime getting eventual access to additional oil reserves in Iraq.

So Bush senior and Clinton made the best of a bad job, hoping that Saddam Hussein would eventually comply with the UN requirements over WMD. As soon as he had done so, he could have been rehabilitated into the international community and the oil refineries could get back to work fully. His evil acts could even be forgotten. After all, in 1983 President Reagan had referred to the Soviet Union as the 'evil empire', but by 1987, under the new leadership of Mikhail Gorbachev, he had negotiated a nuclear disarmament agreement with the Soviet Union, and Gorbachev had become more popular in US opinion polls than Reagan himself. A week is a long time in politics.

But Saddam Hussein didn't take the hint. He continued his policy of cheat and retreat over the WMD. We have no clear idea why – giving in would certainly have saved a lot of people, including himself, a lot of trouble.

It's a possibility that the current President Bush may see himself as completing some kind of family business. It would certainly fit with his tendency to personalise power: to see countries simply as the extension of the person running them. This is a common failure among many egotistical politicians around the globe, who like to overemphasise the role of the individual in running a country.

This theory also contains the implication that if Saddam Hussein could be removed, then all would be well in Iraq, if not the wider Middle East. Clearly that optimism was wrong. Getting rid of one problem has only created others.

Bush was influenced by neo-conservatives and the Project for a New American Century

This is the most controversial theory of the eight. It argues that President Bush – who knows little about foreign policy – is highly influenced by a group of colleagues who have a radical agenda for America's role in the world. The NGO the Project for a New American Century (PNAC) was formed in 1997, while President Clinton was in power. It involved such figures as the current US Vice President, Dick Cheney, Defence Secretary Donald Rumsfeld and World Bank President Paul Wolfowitz (see website: http://www.newamericancentury.org).

In September 2000, prior to the November presidential election won by George Bush, PNAC issued its strategic plan on how America should exercise global leadership and project its military power, arguing that now the Soviet Union had disappeared, the US should ensure its global domination for decades to come. PNAC wanted, among other things, a massive increase in military expenditure, new generations of nuclear weapons and better protection of the US homeland. After Bush won the presidential election in November 2000, some of the authors of PNAC's plan were recruited into the Bush Administration.

September 11 2001 was the turning point for PNAC: a new sense of urgency created the opportunity for its agenda to be put into effect with greater speed. One of its targets was Saddam Hussein. Within days of September 11, some of Bush's colleagues were talking of going after Saddam Hussein – even though he wasn't involved in the attacks. They wanted to remake the political landscape in the Middle East and they would start with Iraq.

The term 'neo-conservative' means a new type of

conservative. Neo-conservatives acquired this label because some of them started on the left of the political spectrum and moved right. But I don't think it's a very helpful term, because some of the neo-conservatives' greatest critics are traditional conservatives. The neo-conservatives certainly aren't funded by the traditional conservative American philanthropists.

A traditional conservative wants to preserve what he or she sees as worthwhile qualities or activities in a world of rapid change. In terms of foreign policy, most American conservatives want to retain the American tradition – established by the first President, George Washington – of keeping out of the affairs of other countries. This is the longest continuous theme in US foreign policy. The US liberated itself from Britain during the 1776–83 American Revolution and had no desire to get involved in running the affairs of other countries.

Some business interests shared that conservatism. Wars cost money and increase government power over the daily lives of citizens and corporations. Traditional conservatives in the business world believed wars were a waste of money – and a potential loss of customers. They weren't too keen on money being spent on social welfare programs in the US, so they certainly didn't want it going overseas.

While running for president in 2000, Bush complained about the 'nation-building' activities of the Clinton Administration, such as the peacekeeping work in the Balkans. He promised not to get involved in such costly activities if elected. Now Bush is involved in a bigger nation-building activity than Clinton ever attempted. Why the change? Because of the influence of the neo-conservatives.

Neo-conservatives want a far more active global role for America. They see America as an exceptional country whose values should be exported to others for the benefit of the world. Hollywood already exports its values so why not send democracy and capitalism out there as well? Neo-conservatives' heroes include Democrat Presidents Woodrow Wilson (one of the founders of the League of Nations after World War I) and Franklin Roosevelt (who led the country during World War II). Ronald Reagan – who began as a Democrat before deciding he'd do better as a Republican – was another hero, until he started to go easy on Gorbachev's Soviet Union.

Neo-conservatives want to end the American tradition of isolationism and keeping out of other countries' affairs. Instead, they think they know what's best for other countries. They saw Saddam Hussein's Iraq as a good starting place for recreating the world order, and hope that a flourishing democratic Iraq will be a model for other Arab countries and Iran – that there will be, to use an old expression, a 'domino effect' of one Middle Eastern country after another moving to democracy.

Traditional conservatives have a low opinion of what any government can achieve. They would prefer as small a government as possible and leave as much as possible to the decisions of individuals and the market. Neo-conservatives have a far greater belief in the power of government – even if some of the government services get outsourced to the business sector. They believe that governments should set the national direction; more specifically, the US Government.

The War on Terrorism has given the US Government unprecedented peacetime powers over the US homeland and American citizens – and now the Bush Administration is doing the same in Iraq.

This is the longest-lasting of the eight hypotheses, but personally I remain unsure as to why President Bush invaded Iraq.

Countries go to war for strange reasons

Human beings don't seem to learn much from history. Here are two bizarre case studies: the first shows how Britain went to war over an ear, and the second explains how the US went to war in Vietnam partly over an attack that never took place.

The War of Jenkins' Ear (1739–42)

On 19 October 1739 the British went to war against Spain over an incident in 1731 when a British sailor's ear was cut off.

In 1738, British sea captain Robert Jenkins testified before the British Parliament that in 1731, while sailing his ship, the *Rebecca*, in the Caribbean, he was captured by Spanish coastguards who cut off his ear. He showed the politicians his pickled ear as proof. The politicians and the media were outraged, and demanded that Britain go to war against Spain in revenge.

In fact, the loss of Jenkins' ear was not really the reason for the war, but those British politicians and journalists who wanted to go to war needed a cause that would whip up public opinion. The slicing off of a man's ear was a 'human interest' story, something everyone could understand.

The real reasons for the war were wealth, power and territory. The Spanish empire was in decline and Britain was beginning its ascent to global power. This war was part of the politicking manoeuvres by which Britain replaced Spain in parts of the Americas. The Spanish also controlled the West Indies, which were a key part in the balance of world power, because they were the entry point to the valuable Spanish trade market. The Spanish wanted to maintain a monopoly over their trade in their own areas, while the British wanted access to that trade.

But war was not inevitable. By 1739, there had been peace in Britain for about a quarter of a century. Some politicians and financial interests argued that Britain was doing very well out of peace and little could be gained from a war.

On 9 April 1731, a Spanish coastguard ship, the *San Antonio*, intercepted Captain Jenkins' brig *Rebecca* near Havana, on its way from Jamaica to London. According to the Spanish, Jenkins was a smuggler whose cargo did not match what he claimed to be carrying in his log books. They also said that he abused the Spanish crew who caught him. The Spanish punished him by cutting off one of his ears.

Jenkins' supporters claimed that he was an honest merchant captain who'd been brutally abused by Spanish customs officials, and that the removal of his ear was intended as an insult to the British people generally. They demanded that the Spanish nation should be punished – a cry that was taken up by the flourishing newspapers. This was one of the earliest examples of the British going to war as a result of a campaign conducted partly in the media.

But there were some British people who thought the evidence of ill-treatment was weak. They were not pro-Spanish; they just wondered whether they were being told the whole story. After all, there was some doubt as to the legality of Jenkins' activities in the West Indies; he could really have been a smuggler. His ear could have been cut off for other – worse – crimes, or he could have lost it in a street brawl. Furthermore, his ear was cut off in 1731 but it was only in 1738 that the issue was brought before Parliament. Why the delay? Some people even doubted whether the pickled object Jenkins showed the politicians was actually his severed ear.

Nevertheless, Britain declared war on Spain in October 1739. There was simply too much political pressure and public opinion in favour of the war. The War of Jenkins' Ear became absorbed into wider European wars and people soon forgot about the incident.

The Gulf of Tonkin incident

One of the biggest mysteries of the Vietnam War is the 'incident' that triggered it. When US ships were attacked on 4 August 1964 in the Gulf of Tonkin in the South China Sea, US Congress voted to authorise President Johnson to take all necessary measures to repel any armed attack against US forces. It was a blank cheque for the use of force.

But what really happened on 4 August 1964? From what we know now, it seems the 'attack' never took place.

On the night of 2 August, the US destroyer *Maddox*, which was spying on North Vietnam, was attacked by three North Vietnamese patrol torpedo boats. The *Maddox* withdrew. On the night of 4 August, the Pentagon claimed that North Vietnamese boats had again attacked the *Maddox* and a sister destroyer, the *Turner Joy*. Within hours, President Johnson announced on American television that US ships had been attacked by North Vietnamese boats and that he had ordered retaliatory air strikes on North Vietnam. An outraged media, public and Congress wanted immediate action. On 7 August, Congress agreed to authorise the President to take all necessary measures to protect US forces.

In fact, the whole incident was a mistake. On 4 August the *Maddox* returned to the area with the *Turner Joy*. The crews were expecting problems and so were overanxious and overeager. In their nervousness, they mistook the sounds of their own propellers for the sound of enemy boats. The alarm was given and firing commenced. After four hours of 'activity', both ships left the area unharmed.

There were no North Vietnamese ships involved, but the North Vietnamese didn't deny they had attacked the two ships on the second occasion. They were willing to play along because this was a great propaganda gain for them: in the eyes of the world, North Vietnamese ships had driven off US destroyers for the second time. They were willing to take the credit, even if they had not earned it. They became the toast of the Communist world.

President Johnson's advisers, including the US Secretary of Defence, Robert McNamara, used the Gulf of Tonkin incident as the basis of expanding the war. If the media and Congress had done a better job of investigating the incident, the escalation of the Vietnam War could have been avoided. The US military presence in Vietnam in early 1964 was still limited. There was no indication that it would become one of the biggest wars – and most embarrassing defeats – in US history.

Robert McNamara publicly supported the war, but privately he thought it was a mistake and that the US could not win, as he admitted in his memoir in 1995. That same year he visited Vietnam as an honoured guest and in a conversation with the Vietnamese military hero Vo Nguyen Giap discovered that there had been no attack that night – something McNamara had long suspected.

President Johnson didn't create the 'incident' on 4 August; it really was an accident. But he made the most of the incident for his own purposes and the gullible politicians and media played along. By the time the US pulled out of Vietnam in 1975, over a million Vietnamese and 58,000 Americans had been killed – along with 504 Australians.

10

❓ What is 'globalisation'?

The current world order is ending but there is no clear replacement for it. The old order is based on nation-states (countries) with centralised national governments. It has worn well but now it's wearing out. Instead, we're seeing the erosion of national boundaries and the reduced significance of national governments. We're becoming a world without borders. The process of globalisation is now the most important factor in world politics.

We can break globalisation down into five key features:

1. The new era is 'global' rather than 'international'. The concept 'international' regards the nation-state as the basic component of world affairs, so everything that happens at the planetary level is a form of interaction between nation-states or national governments. That's no longer the case.

There are other – non-nation-state – actors on the world stage: most notably, transnational corporations, intergovernmental organisations (particularly the United Nations) and non-governmental organisations (such as the women's, peace and environment movements).
2. The process of globalisation isn't a sinister conspiracy organised by a group of transnational corporations or evil individuals wishing to take over the world. It is simply another evolution in the world's affairs.
3. The lessening of the power of national governments is creating a vacuum at the global level, which isn't being filled by any supra-national organisation. There's no clear replacement for the existing world order – or even an agreed mechanism for creating one.
4. The process of globalisation is not reversible. It's not possible to reinvent the era of nation-states. We have to come to terms with the new era and begin searching for a new order, rather than waste time trying to patch up the system of nation-states. Countries will still exist, but the process of globalisation means that national governments will have to share their power with three other groups of entities – transnational corporations, intergovernmental organisations and non-governmental organisations.
5. Globalisation is more than just a matter of economics. The process of globalisation has happened so swiftly that global change is running ahead of governments' ability to manage it. Economics is only one part of that process.

Economic globalisation

There are several main forms of globalisation. Economic globalisation refers to the growing importance of transnational corporations. A transnational corporation is a company that engages in foreign direct investment and owns, or controls, activities in more than one country. Transnational corporations are now the main global economic force. They sprawl across national political boundaries, thereby eroding the notion of a national economy and creating a global one. Transnational corporations are now the major driving forces in economic policy. Corporations can, for example, move jobs offshore in search of lower costs, cheaper workers and fewer unions. They can also change character to maximise profits. For instance, if a government tries to protect its own industries by keeping out imports, the transnational corporation will try to buy companies in that country and so produce its goods 'locally'.

Transnational corporations have evolved through four stages. The first stage, from about 1895 to 1945, saw the emergence and consolidation of oligopolies – a small number of large corporations dominating a market – in key sectors in North America, Western Europe and Japan. During the second stage, from 1946 to the mid-1960s, transnational corporations rose to their current position of prominence and were responsible for roughly 80 per cent of the trade conducted outside the Communist bloc.

The third stage, from the mid-1960s to the present, has seen the corporations consolidate their dominance. For example, there have been mergers across national boundaries, and a rise in the significance of non-US corporations, such as additional Japanese and Western European ones.

The fourth stage is the current process of consolidation with the opening up of the former Soviet bloc to transnational corporations. China is also more willing to welcome foreign corporations' investment. Virtually the entire globe is now within reach of the corporations. There's a new oil rush taking place right now, with corporations eager to get into countries that were largely off limits during the Cold War – such as Kazakhstan, the Russian Arctic Circle, China's Tarim Basin and the waters off Vietnam. Former Communist countries are also opening up to the capital, technology and management skills that international oil firms offer, and foreign oil corporations are keen to resume exploration in Libya now that international sanctions against it have been lifted.

Another development that fosters globalisation is the staffing of transnational corporations by a kind of global 'civil service'. Corporations have been far more successful than the United Nations in encouraging their employees to see themselves as global workers. They've been able to create a commitment to a single, unified global mission that transcends nationalistic feelings by individual staff. For example, workers don't think of themselves as being employed by a Japanese car maker trying to build and sell its products in the US. Instead, such a person works for Honda or Nissan or Toyota.

The telecommunications revolution means that workers can be employed in cheap labour areas to carry out data processing for an entire corporation. Swissair, for example – a corporation with its headquarters in Switzerland – has created an affiliate in India to handle revenue accounting functions for the corporation as a whole. Similarly, a New York insurance corporation has relocated all its data processing to Ireland. The time-zone difference in this instance is a huge advantage, because it allows the New York office to offer an overnight service: the paperwork is processed in Ireland during its working day and a cheque is ready for collection the following day New York time. For the same reason, British Telecom has relocated some of its administration, finance, personnel, and customer service operations to Australia. While the northern hemisphere sleeps, Australian staff work on software development, fixing problems that occurred during the day in the European and UK network. A company in Wellington, New Zealand, is exploiting time-zone differences to create a 'niche market' in translating documents in foreign languages. The documents are sent by email from Europe, translated overnight in Wellington and emailed back so that they are ready the following day.

In the 1950s, transnational corporations were widely regarded as a peculiarly US form of business organisation. But by the early 1990s, they were commonplace – every industrialised country provided a base for them. Collectively, transnational corporations were becoming the dominant form of organisation responsible for the international exchange of goods and services.

Public order globalisation

Another main form of globalisation is 'public order globalisation'. This has developed out of the increasing need for governments to work together on common problems. Diseases, pollution and climate changes don't recognise national boundaries; they have no respect for lines on maps.

National governments work together through intergovernmental organisations such as the United Nations and European Union. Until the recent expansions of the UN's peacekeeping work, about 80 per cent of the UN's expenditure was on economic and social cooperation. This kind of work is done out of the public eye, with little publicity and political controversy. For example, even though the US and Soviet Union were enemies during the Cold War, their respective allies were working together on various projects. The World

Health Organization's program to eradicate smallpox was based on a Soviet proposal and the project was headed by an American. The International Telecommunications Union (ITU) oversaw the creation of the global telephone dialling service, based on numbers rather than letters, which led to international subscriber dialling (ISD). The ITU also oversaw the conference process by which radio and television airwaves were apportioned out. The International Maritime Organization created a common bill of lading for merchant marine vessels; and the World Meteorological Organization created a global network for exchanging data on weather patterns.

These may seem like unexciting developments compared with the mass media's interest in war and the arms race, but their benefits have had a lasting significance. The Cold War has come and gone but the contribution of the less glamorous functional cooperation remains. Indeed, with the Cold War over, there are now far more opportunities to telephone or trade across national borders.

People's globalisation

People's globalisation is the third main form of globalisation. It is the mobilisation of people power and is achieved mainly through non-governmental organisations (NGOs), such as Amnesty International, the women's movement, the peace movement and Rotary International. They enable people to work together across national borders for the betterment of humankind.

NGOs are the most powerful way of focusing attention on a problem and mobilising public opinion. The 1972 UN Conference on the Environment arose largely from various

NGOs' arguments that there was an environmental crisis – such as the Club of Rome report on the 'limits to growth', which became the biggest-selling environment book in history. The NGOs acted – and governments had to react. Similarly, NGOs publicised the Brundtland Report on the environment and development, and so encouraged governments and the UN to create the 1992 Conference on Environment and Development (UNCED).

NGOs are a growing force in global politics. They appeal to people who are disenchanted with the usual party political process, provide a sense of vision and continuity that outlasts the short-term perspective of governments, and are adept at attracting media coverage for their causes.

11

? Is globalisation good or bad?

This is a difficult question to answer because it's so broad. Some aspects of globalisation may be good and some may be bad. It's a bit like asking: is rain good or bad? If I was a farmer I'd probably want rain, but if I was planning a picnic in the park I'd rather it remained fine.

In essence the world is moving into an era when national boundaries are no longer important. 'Globalisation' refers to the declining power of national governments generally.

As discussed in the question 'How many countries are there in the world and how are they created?', national governments are a comparatively new idea. International lawyers date them from 1648, when the Thirty Years' War in Europe ended resulting in the Treaty of Westphalia (hence the name of the present world order: the 'Westphalian System').

Prior to that time, people in Europe lived in small tribes, possibly as part of a large empire. No one suddenly decided to create the Westphalian System in 1648; it was only with the benefit of hindsight that people could see a new world order had been created. Peoples ('nations') were now to be governed by 'states' – that is, political, legal and military systems of administration – so creating the concept of nation-states. As the Europeans colonised the world, they took this system with them. The nation-state system is now so prevalent that it is seen as the norm in world politics. The United Nations currently has 191 nation-state members, with East Timor as the most recent member. If President Bush is successful with his Middle East 'road map for peace', then Palestine will be the next nation-state to join the UN. But the process of globalisation means that national governments are no longer so relevant to world politics. If an alien from outer space arrived on Earth and said 'Take me to your leader', where would we take it? To John Howard? George Bush? Bill Gates? Rupert Murdoch?

Transnational corporations are now the major player in world economics: they – rather than national governments – set the pace of economic change. Anti-globalisation demonstrators are right to identify the problems that some corporations create, but this is a debate we should have had decades ago – before the horse bolted from the stable. The debate should have been based on people acquiring simpler lifestyles, but now people are addicted to consumerism. For better or worse, we enjoy a consumption-dominated lifestyle, and few consumers will revert back to simpler, less extravagant tastes. The corporations have a grip over our tastes and lifestyles.

The globalisation trend does have some positive developments. Another form of globalisation is the anti-globalisation movement itself. 'People power' movements – NGOs or civil society organisations – are a way for people to work together to make a better world. Such people are disenchanted with politicians because they have so little power and have decided to set their own agenda. Examples of people power include Amnesty International, Greenpeace, Médecins Sans Frontières (Doctors Without Borders) and the International Commission of Jurists.

In a way, anti-globalisation demonstrators are as much a part of the globalisation process as the people and organisations they criticise. But it's 'people power globalisation' versus 'economic globalisation'. For example, the anti-globalisation movement operates very effectively in cyberspace. It knows how to use the international mass media to play to a global audience, and some of its members fly overseas for demonstrations. The movement also draws on members' individual experiences, turning them into cumulative learning experiences: building on lessons from previous demonstrations, such as in Seattle in 1999 when activists disrupted the World Trade negotiations. It's also tapping into the worldwide worries that some people – such as unemployed workers – have about globalisation. Generally, then, the anti-globalisation activities have been a successful form of globalisation.

Another beneficial aspect of globalisation is 'public order globalisation': where governments work together to combat pollution, disease or climate change – all problems a country is unable to solve alone. A country may have a fine record in environmental protection, for example, but this will be of little value if it is living downwind of a dirty country. Governments may not wish to collaborate on such issues, but they have little choice: they either work together or perish separately.

This kind of work is also called 'functional cooperation': getting experts to work together out of the public eye. Politicians like to approach every issue with an open mouth – take the current negotiations over the Middle East, for example – but technicians from different countries can quietly knit the world together in a system of mutually beneficial arrangements, such as the standardisation of telephone systems mentioned earlier or the exchange of information on diseases and weather.

The UN does this kind of work all day every day, via its specialised bodies such as the World Health Organization, the UN Environmental Programme, the International Maritime Organization and the UN Children's Fund. If the UN disappeared today, we would have to reinvent it to perform all these basic tasks that we take for granted.

We see there are many beneficial aspects to globalisation. The trouble is, governments haven't done enough to explain to their citizens what globalisation entails. But if they did, some citizens might start wondering why we bother having national politicians and national politics at all – they're not so relevant in the new era. In the meantime, we see activists such as the anti-globalisation movement and individuals like Pauline Hanson taking advantage of this information vacuum.

Globalisation isn't going to go away; it's the main game in town. The anti-globalisation demonstrations are useful as a way of drawing attention to the importance of globalisation, but what we need now are some ideas for how Australia is going to make the most of this new global era. One plan is to set up a Commission for the Future, to help stimulate national debate on where Australia – and the globe – is heading.

The paradoxes of globalisation

Globalisation presents many national challenges. Here are three of them.

1. The more a government deregulates the national economy, the less scope it has to direct where it's going.

The more deregulation there is, the more a country is exposed to outside influences. 'Deregulation' means that a government reduces its role in the national economy such as by selling off its assets (like Qantas or the Commonwealth Bank) or stops trying to control the economy (for example, private ownership of gold bars was once tightly controlled and there were restrictions on how much Australian and foreign currency a person could take out of the country).

2. The overall process of globalisation has continued irrespective of which political party is in power.

Throughout the 1980s, conservative parties were in power in the US and UK, and Labor parties were in power in Australia and New Zealand. Nevertheless all four countries introduced similar policies. Politicians come and go, but globalisation remains.

In Australia, the controversial issue of banking deregulation would have gone ahead irrespective of which party won the 1983 federal election. The basis of deregulation was set out in an inquiry chaired by the late Sir Keith Campbell. It was created in 1979 by the Fraser Government and reported in 1981. Some of its reforms were under way by the time of the 1983 election. The Campbell Report was rejected by the majority of the Labor Party, including Hawke and

Keating, for its free-market dogma. However, once in office, Hawke, Keating and most of the Labor Party underwent a conversion. The politicians were convinced by their better-informed advisers that deregulation was the best option.

Nonetheless, it is ironic that the Labor Government of the 1980s deregulated the banking system, when a previous Labor Government (1941–49) almost nationalised it. R.G. Casey (a Liberal politician) raised 100,000 pounds in the UK – where three of the banks had their head offices – to mount a successful legal challenge to the legislation in the Australian High Court and the Privy Council in London. Then again, the Labor Government in the 1980s was very different from the Labor Government in the 1940s – if only because the global conditions were very different.

3. *Nationalism on the one hand; globalisation on the other.*

The Labor Government of the 1980s fostered a sense of Australian nationalism, and when Paul Keating was Prime Minister he talked about the need for Australia to become a republic. Meanwhile, the process of globalisation was reducing the range of options available to any Australian government regarding the Australian economy, to the point that Australia is no longer master of its economic destiny. The economic development of Australia since 1946 owes much to foreign investment in its mines, factories and offices. Foreign ownership in Australia is as high as 70 or 80 per cent in industries like petroleum, cars, and chemicals, for example; 50 per cent in mining; and about 30 per cent in manufacturing.

12

❓ Why are African children starving?

Most African children aren't starving. If they were, they would be dead by now. People can't keep on starving; they die after only a few weeks. But the question raises two interesting issues:

1. What is the food situation in Africa?
2. Why do we have a persistent image of starving children in Africa?

What is the food situation in Africa?

The traditional statement about food availability is that there's enough food for everyone, but a shortage of money to

Why are African children starving?

pay for it. This is much like the great Irish famine in the 1840s: there was food around, but the Irish were too poor to buy it.

Nowadays, however, there's a growing concern that the world may be running out of food. The world has over 6 billion people, so there's a problem with population growth. Half of the world's annual population growth of 77 million people occurs in only six countries: India, China, Pakistan, Nigeria, Bangladesh and Indonesia. Each country with a growing population faces a risk of losing agricultural land on a per capita basis. Each will need to rely increasingly on grain imports.

Overall, there's a global trend towards the loss of agricultural land. For thousands of years, until the middle of the twentieth century, there was a steady increase in the area of land under cultivation. Now, for the first time in human history, the area under cultivation is starting to be reduced.

Urban sprawl is one explanation for the loss of farmland. There's also the problem of industrialisation, not least in China where roads, houses and factories are being built on good farming land. China's annual grain production is now declining each year in absolute terms.

Africa has its own problems. People there are often malnourished: they're not necessarily starving but at the same time they're not getting enough food. They have weakened immune systems and so are vulnerable to diseases. Many children can't study at the schools that do exist because their minds are occupied with their lack of food.

Let's take Rwanda as an example. Rwanda is Africa's most densely populated country. Between 1950 and 1990 the population tripled from 2.1 million to 6.8 million. This contributed to land degradation, deforestation and famine; in turn, these stresses ignited the undercurrent of ethnic strife that led to the 1994 genocide in which 800,000 people were killed. During that time, the daily rate of death was actually higher than the Nazis achieved in the Holocaust. The population of Rwanda now stands at 8.1 million. It's only a matter of time before the ethnic stresses start again.

Africa has major problems with producing enough food for all its people. But if it has to import food, how will it pay for it?

Meanwhile, with most of the planet's arable land already under cultivation and with additional cropland being built on, there's little chance that the world grain area will be able to rebound. How will we feed all the extra people in Africa and beyond?

Why do we have a persistent image of starving children in Africa?

The use of the image of starving children is one of the most sensitive internal debates among charities raising funds to send to developing countries, and one that often pitches the public relations/marketing and donor branches against the information and research branches.

The basic problem is that people give money from the heart, not from the head. They're not necessarily interested in high-flown rational discussions about why children are malnourished, the impact of free trade, the World Bank and the IMF. They respond emotionally to images of starving children.

The dilemma for aid agencies is whether they should use images of starving children to raise funds. It has often been customary to include a picture of a starving child in the corner of a newspaper advertisement with a coupon to cut out to send in with the donation. On the one hand, such images are often successful in tugging at the heartstrings of potential donors. Happy, smiling children don't evoke the same sense of urgency and a desire to help. They seem to be doing very well already without the need for a donation, is the thought.

On the other hand, the images reinforce public perception that Africa is just a continent of starving children, when there's much more to Africa than starvation. Additionally, the images become self-defeating after a while, contributing to a sense of donor fatigue, whereby potential donors are tired of seeing the same old images and hearing about the same old disasters. People may be inclined to give up hope of progress ever being made in the continent, thinking that nothing seems to work in Africa. Finally, the images can also be demeaning to the people the aid agencies are seeking to help.

The debate goes back and forth; it's a difficult one to resolve. In the meantime, it's not surprising that many people, when they think of Africa, automatically think of disasters and starving children.

13

❓ Why is Australia the United States' most faithful ally?

Australia was the only country in the twentieth century to have fought alongside the US in every war the US was involved in. Not even the UK can claim that record, as it sent no troops to Vietnam. Australia began the twenty-first century maintaining that record, joining the US – and the UK – in the invasion of Iraq in 2003.

Australia's remarkable consistency in this – irrespective of the political party in power – can be explained by dividing Australian foreign and defence policy into the following five themes:

1. Fear of invasion.
2. Poor defence.
3. The need for a protector.

4. The need to provide incentives to help Australia.
5. Lack of popular interest in foreign and defence policy.

Fear of invasion

One of the earliest actions of the British when they first established their settlement at Sydney Cove in 1788 was to build an earthen fort and put a cannon in it. They had found it so simple to seize their first bit of Australia, they were afraid someone else would come along and take it from them just as easily. In those days, Britain's potential enemies were the French and Dutch. Later, they were the Tsarist Russians, Japanese, Germans, Indonesians, Vietnamese and Chinese, and then the Soviet Union.

Fort Victoria, on Thursday Island, was designed as Australia's 'Gibraltar'. Its location in the Torres Strait, north of Queensland, meant that it commanded the naval route around northeast Australia. Responding to the fear of a Russian invasion in 1892, the Queensland Government installed three six-inch guns supported by rapid-fire six-pounders in the fort, with similar batteries at Brisbane and Townsville. Fifty troops of No 3 Company, Queensland Permanent Artillery, were deployed there, but the Russians never came. The fort was closed down in 1925. It was reactivated during World War II as a lookout post to warn of Japanese air attacks, but is now merely a popular tourist attraction.

This fear of invasion was also a driving force in bringing the Australian colonies together to form the Commonwealth of Australia in 1901. They were worried about Germany's reach into the South Pacific, and still troubled by the Russians. The Commonwealth of Australia's first major military operation was to supply troops to assist Britain in the South African Boer War.

Poor defence

Australia is a big country and there's always been doubt as to whether it could defend itself unaided. This doubt came partly from the inherent fears of the settlers, many of whom came from countries around the world that had military alliances of some sort, and so believed Australia should also forge its own allegiances.

This fixation on the need for alliances has been augmented by concern about the size of the country and its coastline and the comparatively small population available to protect its borders. If just the indented Western Australian coastline were laid out in a straight line, for example, it would stretch two-thirds of the distance from Perth to London. The usual Mercator map projections of Australia fail to show its true comparative size. For instance, Greenland, which appears so large on the Mercator map projection, is much less than the size of Western Australia.

The need for a protector

The concern about Australia's inability to defend itself led in turn to the belief that it needed a protector. Australia set up a kind of insurance policy, whereby it would provide troops and other facilities to its protector in the hope that the protector would reciprocate in a time of Australia's need.

Australia's first protector, from 1788 to 1941, was the United Kingdom. During World War II, however, the

Australian Government became aware that its war priorities differed markedly from those of the UK. When Japan entered the conflict with its attack on Pearl Harbor on 7 December 1941, followed by the invasion of the Kra Isthmus ports and consequent sweep southwards towards Singapore, which fell on 14 February 1942, it became clear that the Japanese forces posed a grave danger to British colonies in Asia, including Australia. British policy, however, remained focused on the need to beat Germany first. The British empire was suffering 'imperial overstretch': it was too big, too unwieldy and too spread out. It couldn't cope with threats in both Europe and Asia at the same time.

Ironically, as we now know, Australia was never under any threat of invasion from Japan during World War II. The 1981 Australian Parliamentary Joint Committee on Foreign Affairs and Defence Report, *Threats to Australia's Security – Their Nature and Probability*, includes information from a March 1942 Japanese military report that rejects invasion. The Japanese estimated it would require twelve army divisions for an invasion (which I assume to be around 240,000 total personnel), necessitating 1,500,000 tons of shipping as well as the protection of the main body of the fleet with air cover, which would reduce the personnel deployed on other fronts. Also, the 'national character' of Australians meant they 'would resist to the end'.

After Pearl Harbor, however, Australia came to see its priorities were more in line with a substantial body of opinion within the US Government, rather than with the UK. This realisation changed the entire basis of Australian foreign and defence policy. Since World War II, although Australia has retained its traditional links with the British monarchy, the US has replaced the UK as Australia's foreign policy mentor.

The Australia–US defence relationship has been formalised via a series of military treaties. For many years, the main treaty, concluded in September 1951, was the Security Treaty between Australia, New Zealand and the US (ANZUS). But ANZUS is now in limbo, owing to New Zealand's opposition to nuclear-powered and nuclear-armed US warships visiting its marine ports. Even before the mid-1980s, when New Zealand first introduced its nuclear-free policy, there was some doubt over the full military significance of the treaty as it didn't include a specific commitment by any party immediately to assist another in the event of an attack. Over the years, the Australia–US military relationship has been augmented by other, more specific agreements.

Australia initially insisted on the creation of the ANZUS treaty as the price the US had to pay for Australia's support for a peace treaty between the US and Japan. Life is full of ironies, however: Japan hasn't returned to its policy of militarism; instead, it is now Australia's major trading partner.

What did the US get out of this relationship with Australia? During the Cold War, the US regarded the South Pacific as a comparatively minor theatre of operations: there was hardly any Soviet presence there, civilian or military. Cuba, Europe, Africa and Asia were seen as far more important.

In practical terms, of course, Australia could be relied upon to support the US. For instance, Australia would never have invaded Iraq in 2003 if the US hadn't done so. Also, a great deal of foreign and defence policy is based on routine small matters rather than the high drama reported in the mass media. Australia has long viewed its own daily foreign and defence matters through the Washington prism, with the US setting the priorities.

This type of small detail often comes to light in memoirs published long after the event. Australian politician Clyde Cameron noted in his diary (later published as *The Cameron Diaries* in 1990) Australia's experience on a UN voting matter. When Cameron was an observer on the Australian delegation at the UN in 1976, he saw the Australian ambassador being obliged by the US to back down on a policy devised within the Australian mission. Cameron said he had no doubt that the Americans gave instructions to their embassy in Canberra to put the necessary pressure on the Department of Foreign Affairs; or, better still, to contact Prime Minister Fraser about the matter. And as a result, Australia changed its policy.

The need to provide incentives to help Australia

Australian politicians, especially in the twentieth century, had few illusions about the reliability of their protector. They may have seen themselves as part of the great British race encircling the globe, but Australia's geographical distance from the UK – and later the US – meant its protection wasn't assured.

Since 1788 Australia has been part of the world's major trading system. The trading system was taken over by the UK around the time of the Industrial Revolution and was drastically overhauled from its Spanish/Portuguese/Dutch predecessors, and then the US took it over from the UK around the time of World War II. Australia was, then, locked into that system from the outset of colonialism.

Britain wasn't just another overseas country for Australia; it was Australia's best customer and main supplier. In fact, Britain was never even really a foreign country – after all, for the first half of the twentieth century it issued Australians with their passports.

Australia never acquired this tight a relationship with the US after 1945. But in economic terms, Australian governments were anxious for US investment alongside the continuation of the UK contribution. All these economic developments helped improve the Australian standard of living, but they also gave the UK and US an incentive to defend Australia, if only to protect their own interests.

This reasoning would also now apply to Japan. Various Australian governments managed to overcome Australian wartime memories of Japanese atrocities to encourage Japanese investment in Australia. Japan does not have a military force to be deployed to defend Australia, but any country contemplating invading Australia – the popular fear has been Indonesia – would also damage Japanese investments in Australia, so the invading country might be restrained by the fear of Japanese economic retaliation.

Lack of popular interest in foreign and defence policy

The problem with Australian defence is that there's no local problem. Australia is the richest country in the region; it has an internationally respected defence force and it's an island continent with one of the most formidable natural defences in the world, such as rugged cliffs and mangrove swamps. It has no serious conflict of interests with any of its neighbours and there are no foreseeable disputes likely to arise well beyond this decade. There is no obvious enemy.

Apart from a brief fear of invasion in 1942–43, Australia has not been invaded since 1788. The 1981

Parliamentary report, *Threats to Australia's Security – Their Nature and Probability*, said that only two countries had the military capacity to invade Australia: the US and USSR. The former is an ally, and the latter lacked any need to do so. The USSR had little to gain from invading Australia since it was largely self-sufficient in raw materials. Ironically, Australia was only a nuclear target because of the US bases on its soil.

Indonesia, as the 1981 report pointed out, did not have the capacity to invade Australia. Indeed, having invaded East Timor in 1975, it had great difficulty subduing resistance to the invasion even on that small island, from poor people who lacked a national defence force. Three decades later, that assessment still stands. Indonesia has even more domestic issues to address (although it is no longer occupying East Timor) with local insurgencies from Aceh in the west to West Papua in the east.

With no obvious enemy, then, Australians have shown a general lack of interest in traditional foreign and defence policy issues. Interest has been kindled at times of great emergency (almost always a war), but there's never been a determined follow-through of interest. In the meantime, like a householder with insurance cover, most Australians have been unconcerned about foreign policy since they knew – or at least hoped – that the insurance company (the UK or more recently the US) would come good in the event of a crisis. And given the region's comparative tranquillity – as far as Australia has been concerned – there's been no need to activate the policy.

14

What are the disadvantages of Australia's traditional foreign and defence policy?

There have been three disadvantages to the 'protector' approach to Australian foreign and defence policy:

1. The extent of the premiums, namely the supply of Australian forces.
2. Australia's direct military and political links with the US reduce its foreign policy options.
3. Australia's reliance upon 'great and powerful friends' and 'insurance arrangements' has engendered intellectual laziness.

The extent of the premiums

Since at least 1885, Australian troops have been deployed in wars fought by the UK or, more recently, the US. During

World War I, more Australian troops per capita were killed than Belgian troops, even though the war was fought partly on Belgian soil. While Australia sent comparatively few troops to Vietnam, it did send some – which is more than can be said for almost all the US's other allies around the world.

Australia's direct military and political links with the US reduce its foreign policy options

Even today, there is a tendency for each foreign policy issue to be viewed in light of the larger framework of Australia's need to maintain friendly relations with the US. Consequently, Australian foreign policy is often made, in general terms, in Washington DC rather than in Canberra. The decision to invade Iraq is a perfect example.

Australia's reliance upon 'great and powerful friends' and 'insurance arrangements' has engendered intellectual laziness

Too often Australia has tended to have slogans in place of foreign policies. 'Anti-Communism', for example, was a slogan but hardly a detailed policy. What Australia needed was a detailed strategy on what it should do in the world to further its own national interest – and not have those interests defined by the UK or US. This should have included more public debate on Australia's foreign role. For example, the government could have provided funds for non-governmental organisations to run educational campaigns.

15

❓ Is the United Nations a world government?

No. The UN is not a 'world government' and is a long way from ever becoming one. On paper, the UN system looks highly impressive. In reality, however, it's under-resourced and therefore its powers are limited.

The UN comprises six 'principal organs': the General Assembly, the Security Council, the International Court of Justice (ICJ), the Economic and Social Council (ECOSOC), the Trusteeship Council, and the Secretariat.

General Assembly

This is the world's main political forum. It meets for more or less the last four months of each year, with all UN member-nations (now 191) present. The General Assembly is the global debating chamber, but not the global parliament because it doesn't pass 'laws'. It adopts resolutions that indicate how the world's governments think on particular issues, but these resolutions are not binding (except in relation to domestic UN affairs) and governments are not obliged to follow them. Indeed, a government may even vote for a resolution and then ignore it: for example, most developed countries refuse to increase their foreign aid to developing countries to the level they have endorsed in General Assembly resolutions.

Security Council

The Security Council is designed to meet day or night to handle threats to international peace and security. Its core currently consists of the Permanent 5, which were the Allied leaders in World War II: the US, Russia, the UK, France and China. Another ten countries serve on the council, in two-year terms, and are elected via the UN's caucus system to maintain a representative balance of the world.

The original vision for the Security Council is underpinned by the ghost of Adolf Hitler, who died only two months before the San Francisco conference finalised the UN Charter. If, the reasoning went, enough nations had worked together in the League of Nations, then Hitler would have been deterred from his aggressive foreign policy. Consequently, the successor to the League of Nations, the UN, was given immense power – on paper, at least.

All UN member-nations agree to be bound by Security Council resolutions – the only part of the UN system with such power – and all member-nations 'shall hold immediately available' defence forces to be deployed as required by the Security Council. A Military Staff Committee was created, drawn from the representatives of the Chiefs of Staff of the five permanent members, to coordinate the Security Council's military operations. But because of the Cold War, this elaborate system was never used. Instead, there evolved an ad hoc system of peacekeeping for intervention in disputes.

The end of the Cold War has seen a great increase in the UN's peacekeeping work; in fact, the UN is now mounting more peacekeeping operations than at any other time in its history. But this is still all improvised, and not according to the elaborate system laid down in 1945.

International Court of Justice

The International Court of Justice (ICJ) is the world's main legal body. Its roots go back about a century, when it was hoped that wars might be avoided if governments were encouraged to use an international court to settle their disputes.

The ICJ has indeed been able to settle some disputes and avoid what could have become international conflicts, but it isn't a 'court' in the same sense as a court of the Australian legal system, for example. An individual who is alleged to have committed an offence is obliged by Australian law to attend a court hearing. If he or she refuses to attend, that in itself is an offence.

By contrast, government attendance at the ICJ is not compulsory. Only about a third of the UN's membership accept its jurisdiction, and, because of national sovereignty, no government can be forced to accept any international obligation. To put it another way, governments are within their rights if they refuse to have anything to do with the ICJ. For example, Australia is in dispute with East Timor over the seabed boundary and has advised the ICJ that it will not accept its jurisdiction to sort out the dispute. Because of national sovereignty, Australia has a right to do this – although some Australians regard its action as immoral.

Trusteeship Council

The Trusteeship Council oversaw the work of the countries administering Trust Territories to ensure that the territories were put on the road to independence. As the World War II Axis colonies (Germany, Italy and Japan) have been given independence, the Trusteeship Council has worked itself out of a job.

Most wars in history have resulted in the winner taking some of the loser's land – indeed, that may have been the reason for going to war in the first place. United States President Woodrow Wilson encouraged the Allies to agree that World War I would be different; the colonies of the losers would not be absorbed into the colonies of the winners. Instead, those colonies would become 'mandated' territories, with a view to their being put on the road to independence.

German New Guinea, for example, was captured by Australia in World War I, as mentioned in 'The process of European colonisation'. It became a mandate in the 1920s and 1930s, and after World War II it became a UN trust territory. It was merged with the Australian colony of Papua, and the nation-state of Papua New Guinea became an independent country in 1975.

Japan, which was an Allied country in World War I, lost its colonies after World II. The mandated territories and the Japanese colonies became, after World War II, 'UN trust territories'.

Economic and Social Council

The Economic and Social Council (ECOSOC) initiates reports and makes recommendations to the General Assembly, UN member-nations and specialised agencies on economic, social and cultural matters. There are sixteen autonomous specialised agencies, some of which are well known to the general public, such as the World Health Organization (WHO), the UN Educational, Scientific and Cultural Organization (UNESCO) and the International Maritime Organization (IMO). There are also the big financial agencies of the World Bank and the International Monetary Fund (IMF), as well as subsidiary bodies such as the UN Fund for Children (UNICEF).

Until the recent expansion of the UN's peacekeeping work, at least 80 per cent of the UN's money went into the areas under ECOSOC. The sums of money involved are minute, but often highly effective. As discussed in 'Public order globalisation', one example is the World Health Organization's (WHO) coordination of the international campaign to eradicate smallpox. The elimination of smallpox has saved national departments of health millions of dollars because they no longer have to vaccinate their populations against the disease. In other words, countries save more money each year than their total annual contribution to all of WHO's work.

Another UN success story is the eradication of river blindness in Africa through the Onchocerciasis Control Programme. The Onchocerciasis Control Programme – a combination of aerial spraying of insecticides and on-the-ground treatment – is a stunning success story. In future years it will be described as one of the twentieth century's great medical triumphs, similar to smallpox eradication and immunisations for children. Such work gets little media coverage, however, because the mass media are only interested in bad news stories, and so the general public will remain largely unaware of the progress being made.

This type of work is called 'functional cooperation': where specialists meet out of the political spotlight and work together in particular fields on special projects. The UN could make even greater progress on economic and social cooperation if only national governments were more willing to work together.

The Secretariat

The Secretariat, headed by the Secretary-General, supplies the personnel for the main UN bodies. Although the UN is a global organisation, it has about as many public servants as does the state of New South Wales – further proof that the UN is not a world government.

Another limitation on the Secretariat is that the staff need to be a truly international civil service. United Nations staff promise not to take instructions from their national governments, but there is a temptation to maintain close links. The USSR and the former Eastern European bloc staff were the worst examples of how UN staff were controlled by their governments; however, there are signs that this has improved with the ending of the Cold War.

The lower-level staff work hard and promotion is on merit. Unfortunately, some of the senior positions are used by governments as a dumping ground for retired politicians – or even active politicians that governments prefer to have out of the country.

16

❓ Why doesn't the United Nations do more?

As we've seen, the UN isn't a world government; it's simply the world's main 'association' of nation-states. And like all associations, it can only move as fast as its members will allow it to. It seems obvious that the UN should be used a great deal more than it is – after all, if nation-states are no longer able to address global economic and social problems, why not use the UN instead? But governments remain reluctant to surrender some of their power to a form of global authority.

And behind all the rhetoric of a new international era, there are two old problems with the UN: the lack of a central vision and the lack of money. Interwoven into the fabric of these two problems is a third: the principle of sovereign independence – countries can't be coerced into accepting international obligations if they do not want them.

Lack of a central vision

The UN is a decentralised organisation. The General Assembly, Security Council and Secretary-General may attract the daily media coverage, but at least 80 per cent of the UN's work is conducted through specialised agencies, such as UNESCO, WHO and the Food and Agricultural Organization (FAO).

Each agency has its own governing board, which is then linked back to different government departments at the national level. For example, the World Bank's Australian Governor is the Australian Treasurer, who may not share the views of his or her colleague, the Minister for Foreign Affairs, on foreign aid issues.

Each agency has its own membership and so each country may choose which specialised agencies to join. The US resigned from UNESCO in the early 1980s, for example, and took the UK with it. The Reagan Administration was heavily influenced by right-wing non-governmental organisations that wanted the US to pull out of the UN, or at least its agencies. UNESCO was the first target. In fact both countries have since rejoined. Each agency also has its own method of operating and its own objectives. This means that some agencies overlap in the field, with some resulting confusion.

Lack of money

At any one time, most UN members are in arrears in paying their annual subscriptions to the UN. For most of the 1960s to the 1980s the biggest debtor was the Soviet Union; in recent years it's been the US. By the standards of government expenditure, the UN runs on minuscule sums of money. If a government regards something as particularly important, it will find the money for it. By this reckoning, the UN is obviously a low-priority item for most governments.

The total amount of money that goes to the UN each year (with the exception of the loan money which passes through the World Bank) is about US$8 billion. The Council of the City of New York operates with a far larger budget than this; and the world spends much more than US$8 billion a week on defence forces. Via taxes, the average Australian pays the UN the equivalent of the cost of a Big Mac, an apple pie and a Coke (about AU$8) per year.

Each year there are various discussions about how the UN can cut its costs. As Winston Churchill might have said, 'Never before have so many people spoken for so long about so little.'

Overcoming the principle of sovereign independence

It is unwise to rely solely upon national governments to settle problems that are essentially of a global type. Indeed, national pride may actually make the problems worse, because governments prefer to maintain 'face' rather than cooperate with supposed enemies. In recent years, however, we've seen governments being obliged to work together not because they want to, but because they have to. Diseases, plagues, famines and financial crises have acquired a greater global character: these problems now seem to be beyond purely national control or solution. Countries must work together or they will perish separately.

This is highlighted by the spread of malaria. More people in developed countries are now dying from malaria, which is principally a Third World disease. Worldwide there are about 300–500 million cases every year and 3000 children die each day from malaria in Africa. The World Health

Organization (WHO) has an annual research budget of only US$6 million for malaria. Transnational drug corporations estimate that it would cost about US$100 million to research, test and register a new drug, but since no Third World country could afford to buy it, it's not profitable to develop it. Consequently, First World tourists are still using Chloroquine and Maloprim on their exotic travels, but risk encountering mosquitoes that are now resistant to these drugs. Malaria is one of the world's major problems, but is overshadowed by diseases that are far more prevalent in First World countries, such as heart attacks.

UN reform

In March 2005, the UN Secretary-General Kofi Annan tabled yet another report on UN reform. Some changes may come from it, but there are still basic issues to be addressed.

First, the UN is not a high-priority item for governments. The mood of isolationism in the US is often commented upon, but it is worth noting that Australia has resigned from the UN Industrial Development Organization, and Howard Government foreign policy white papers usually have very few references to the UN.

Second, there are different motivations behind the various proposals for UN reform. The UN Secretary-General wants a more effective UN, while many governments simply want a smaller, cheaper one.

Finally, governments are slow to recognise that we're living in a new global era with transnational problems. As we've seen in 'Is globalisation good or bad?', a country may have a good environment record, but that's of little value if it's located near a country with a bad environment record.

There's an increasing need for international cooperation, but governments are unwilling to make the most use of the best system for that cooperation. Australia's real national interest, therefore, is to work through the UN to deal with global problems that it can't solve by itself.

17

❓ Will there ever be peace in Israel/Palestine?

I doubt it. There may be occasional reductions in tension, but I fear there will always be wars and rumours of war.

Not all violence in the Middle East is due to the tensions between Israel and Palestine. The region has long been violent, sitting as it does at the 'crossroads of the world', on the land corridor between Europe and Asia. One of the longest wars of the twentieth century, which ran throughout most of the 1980s, was between Iraq and Iran. Israel had no involvement in that war.

I have three main reasons for pessimism about Israel and Palestine:

1. The role of religion.
2. Thousands of years of mutual suspicion and hostility.

3. Too many people making too many claims on too little land.

The role of religion

Israel/Palestine is central to three world religions: Judaism, Christianity and Islam. Each looks to this land for their heritage; their adherents have been there for the entire length of their respective religions.

The Jews have been on the land for thousands of years. They lost control of the area in AD70, when the last major rebellion took place and the Romans crushed them. They didn't regain control of the land until 1948 when the state of Israel was created.

In the meantime, the land was controlled by others. For many of the centuries before World War I, the land was part of the Ottoman (Turkish) empire, some of which is today Lebanon, Syria and Palestine. During this time, the Islamic heritage was created. The prophet Mohammed is said to have ascended to heaven from the spot where the Jewish temple in Jerusalem once existed. This site is the third most important in Islam (after Mecca and Medina, both in Saudi Arabia).

Christians have been in the area for 2000 years. They occupied it briefly during the medieval Crusades against the Muslims. In World War I, the Ottoman empire sided with Germany. After the Allied forces were victorious, Britain took over control of the Holy Land and held on to it as a League of Nations mandate. In 1948, Britain was pushed out by the violence between Jews and Arabs, and was glad to leave.

Jerusalem, one of the world's oldest and most famous cities, is of particular interest for Judaism, Christianity and Islam. No other city has been as beloved or as fought over as Jerusalem. It remains a focal point for international politics because President Bush's 'road map for peace' has yet to sort out the final status of the city between Israel and the new Palestinian entity.

Some Jewish and fundamentalist Christian religious groups predict the city will be the location of the world's final conflict. Some Jewish groups want to rebuild their temple there, but this would require demolishing the Islamic buildings that have been on the site for 1300 years. Such an action would undoubtedly lead to a global war with Islam. Meanwhile, the late Pope John Paul II called for Jerusalem to become an international city, not governed by Israel or Palestine.

Jerusalem

Jerusalem was an unusual choice for a city as it was not near a seaport or trade route, it lacked an adequate water supply and the surrounding land wasn't good for agriculture. However, its central location between the northern and southern Jewish tribes made it useful in King David's plan about 3000 years ago to unite the people into one kingdom. It was also easy to defend because it was on a high hill and dominated the local territory.

King David brought the Ark of the Covenant to Jerusalem. He wanted to build a temple to house it, but was warned by a prophet that as a warrior with blood on his hands it wouldn't be suitable for him to do so. Instead, his son Solomon, a man of peace, took on that task.

Solomon was responsible for Jerusalem's first golden era. The tribes around Solomon's empire were busy fighting among themselves and so he was able to concentrate on improving his country without the constant fear of invasion. Jerusalem became one of the Middle East's most beautiful cities. But after Solomon died in about 922BC his empire fell apart and the country was divided into two. Surrounding countries had become more organised by this time and started to grab territory.

Nebuchadnezzar, King of Babylon, invaded the city in about 587BC and took most of the inhabitants captive. Solomon's temple was destroyed in the siege and Jerusalem became a place of ruins. Those Jews in exile remembered their wonderful city with fondness and yearned to return to it, but were unable to do so until around 537BC, when King Cyrus of Persia beat the Babylonians.

Jerusalem became a great city again under the tolerant Persian Empire. Then Alexander the Great (356–323BC) swept through the region, beat the Persians and tried to impose Greek thinking and religion. The Jews fought back, which provided an opportunity for a war of independence led by Judas Maccabeus. Jerusalem became the capital of newly independent Judea, but this – the last Jewish kingdom – survived only seventy-six years.

The Romans took over Judea in 63BC, and Jerusalem became one of the Roman empire's administrative centres. The half-Jewish Herod family was installed by the Romans. Herod the Great (37–4BC) was a ruthless fighter, a cunning negotiator and a subtle diplomat, and the Romans liked the way he maintained order among the unruly Jews. Unfortunately, he was also paranoid, fearing that others would try to take his power. He killed his sons and one of his wives and, fearing that the baby Jesus – who had better Jewish roots than his own – would eventually rival his power, tried to have him killed as well.

Herod the Great was a high-taxing, big-spending ruler. He wanted to make Jerusalem one of the wonders of the Middle Eastern world and decided to rebuild the temple to win over Jewish support. His temple was going to be even bigger and grander than Solomon's. Some of the stones used for that massive project are still visible today. Jews were expected to visit the city regularly for religious observances and had to pay a temple tax, which helped Herod finance other major projects.

Jesus first went to Jerusalem as a baby, when his parents took him to the temple. He returned twelve years later as a pilgrim for Passover. The pilgrims attracted traders from all over the Middle East. Caravans brought goods from the Arab world, Persia and India. There were some Greeks still in the area, as a residue from the Greek invasion, and also a few Romans. In short, the Jerusalem of Jesus' day was a rich, active and multicultural city.

But boiling away under the surface there was Jewish anger at the Roman occupation. Finally, the Jews rebelled in AD66. The initial campaign went well but they couldn't beat the Roman empire. The city was destroyed in AD70 and the temple was smashed. Today, the last remaining wall of the temple, the Western Wall, is the holiest site in Judaism.

The Islamic conquest of the land began in 633. The prophet Mohammed was miraculously transported from Mecca to Jerusalem and it was there, from what is now the Dome of the Rock, built on the temple site, that he made his ascent into heaven. Jerusalem was never the capital of any Arab territory but it became important as a shrine to Mohammed.

Attention remains focused still on Jerusalem. The Israeli Government would like international recognition of Jerusalem as the capital of its country, formed in 1948. Some Jews would like to rebuild the temple, but to do so they would need to get control of the Dome of the Rock and destroy it. This would create a flashpoint for Jewish–Islamic tension. Meanwhile, Pope John Paul II called for Jerusalem to become an international city, one governed by neither Israel nor Palestine.

At the time of the first ever Easter, Jerusalem was a centre of tension and political intrigue. Two thousand years later, it is again.

Thousands of years of mutual suspicion and hostility

Jews and Arabs are ancient enemies. Their hostility has not been eased by the interference of other countries in their conflict in more recent times.

Britain's period of control over the land was not a happy one. As part of Britain's attempt to get the US involved in World War I, the British Government said that it viewed with favour the creation of a Jewish home in the Middle East. The statement was made by Lord Balfour, the British Foreign Secretary at the time, and is called the 'Balfour Declaration'. At the same time, Lawrence of Arabia was encouraging the Arabs to rebel against their Ottoman rulers with the promise of getting their own homeland. In yet another deal (kept secret at the time) Britain and France agreed to divide the Ottoman empire among themselves.

In the 1920s and 1930s, both Arabs and Jews pressured Britain to honour its deals. In response to the 'Arab problem', Britain created a number of countries, such as Iraq and Saudi Arabia. The 'Jewish problem' was harder to settle. Arabs were already living in the area where foreign Jews wanted to settle. Meanwhile, in 1933 Hitler came to power in Germany and started persecuting the Jews. The Jews wanted to flee to the British territory as refugees, but the Arabs opposed this. Britain didn't want to annoy the Arab rulers in the countries that had a lot of oil wealth so it stopped the influx of Jews, many of whom were trapped in Europe and killed by Hitler.

After World War II, there was greater international sympathy for the Jewish point of view and so there was more pressure on Britain to change its policy. Britain found it all too complicated – especially because it was already busy winding up other parts of the empire – so it handed the problem over to the United Nations.

The UN agreed that the land should be divided up for both communities, with Jerusalem internationalised under the control of a high commissioner who would be neither Jewish nor Islamic. The Jewish Agency accepted the proposal but the Arab League rejected it. It's worth noting that all subsequent proposals – such as President Bush's 'road map for peace' – have been variations of this proposal.

Britain left the land and the Jews declared their own state. The Arab League attacked but were largely beaten off. The surrounding Arab countries attacked Israel again in 1967 and 1973 in an attempt to destroy it, but were beaten both times.

In 1967, Israel occupied the West Bank (the land in Jordan on the west bank of the River Jordan) and the Gaza Strip (between Israel and Egypt). President Bush's 'road map for peace' is based on Israel's withdrawal from those occupied territories – which would become the new nation-state of Palestine – and the Arab countries' agreement to stop attacking Israel – a 'land for peace' deal.

I am dubious that all Arabs will, in fact, stop attacking Israel. It's extremely difficult to negotiate any sort of peace deal with communities that are so hostile to each other. Any sort of compromise is seen as a sign of weakness. If one side makes a concession to move the negotiations forward, then instead of the other side matching it, that side pushes even harder for its own benefit. This was the problem that negotiators had with Palestinian leader Yasser Arafat: when he was given a little he would try to get even more.

Meanwhile, there are hardliners in both communities that don't believe any lasting deal can be done and so oppose all proposals. Many young Palestinians have little faith in the peace process and so prefer violence. Ideally, politicians should adopt the attitude that the peace process is too important to be derailed by such provocation, but the leaders of both sides know that their respective supporters won't accept that. As soon as an attack takes place, the negotiations are stalled and the peace deal is blocked.

Not enough land to go around

A more basic issue is that there are too many people and too many claims on too little land. The area in contention is about the size of the land between Sydney and Newcastle and out to the Blue Mountains in New South Wales. It's difficult to see how 10 million people can live in such a small area in a self-sufficient way. (The total population of the Sydney–Newcastle region is well over half that figure but they can draw upon the resources of the rest of the country for their sustenance.)

There are about 7500 Israeli settlers living there, surrounded by about 1.3 million Palestinians (about 900,000 of them refugees from previous conflicts with Israel). Defending the embattled settlers is a heavy burden for the Israeli Defence Force and the current Israeli Government would like to withdraw from the Gaza Strip. But the settlers refuse to move and conservative Israelis in Israel itself support their right to stay in the land they claim God gave to the Jews (see *Genesis* 28: 10–15). The West Bank is home to about 3.5 million Palestinians and 400,000 Israeli settlers. Getting those Israelis to pull out will be even more difficult as the West Bank city of Hebron is holy to the Jews.

Countries need clear national boundaries but this won't be the case in the new nation-state of Palestine. This new country's configuration will look like a Swiss cheese, with various Israeli enclaves – with connecting roads – running through the West Bank.

There's also the problem of the final status of Jerusalem. The Israelis want it as their new national capital. The Palestinians want the Old Quarter (the 'Arab' section) as the capital of their new country. The Catholic Church wants it internationalised and so under the control of neither Israel nor Palestine – which doesn't appeal to either side.

The Israeli situation is likely to get even more complicated as Israel is losing the demographic war against the Palestinians. Israel's long-term threat comes not from bombs but from maternity wards. The 4.5 million Palestinians are having more children than the 5.7 million Israelis. This means that the total area of Israel and the occupied territories will eventually contain more Palestinians than Israelis.

18

❓ Is Microsoft more powerful than, say, Poland?

That this question is even asked is an indication of the power of transnational corporations. Clearly a dramatic change has occurred in the last sixty years since the end of World War II. Many financial entities are now so large there are fears they will soon overshadow some small governments. Microsoft's annual sales are larger than the annual gross national products of numerous countries.

In many ways, of course, Poland is still far more powerful than Microsoft. It makes laws for all the people and corporations within its national boundaries; it can put people in prison; it is eligible to stand for election to the UN Security Council and other international organisations; and it can host international sporting events like the Olympic Games. No transnational corporation has any of these powers.

But they have different forms of power. The average Australian is far more affected by Microsoft than by Poland. People need Microsoft a great deal more than they may need particular Polish goods and services. A person could go through their entire life not knowing a thing about Poland – and not caring about it either.

The problem is that we're not comparing like with like. We need to look at the different forms of power, and where and how the power is used. Transnational corporations don't want the burdens of government, such as caring for the sick, elderly and unemployed. Some transnational corporations may make military equipment, but they don't want to get caught up in the messy business of going to war to defend their interests.

Transnational corporations have different aspirations from those of national governments. Governments talk in terms of national pride and patriotism, flags and national anthems. Corporations are concerned about global consumerism: they seek global profits and global reach. National patriotism is only important to corporations when it can be used for marketing purposes.

There's a saying that if you want to do well, sell people what they need; if you want to get rich, sell people what they want. Consumers can't eat a national flag, but they can eat fast food. Therefore, the average person is more likely to want to be a consumer of Microsoft than a citizen of Poland.

19

❓ What is 'blow-back' and how is it significant in United States foreign policy?

Blow-back is a term to describe a policy that eventually results in the opposite of what was intended. It's a problem the US is currently facing as a result of applying the philosophy 'The enemy of my enemy is my friend' to its foreign policy. This foreign policy philosophy has two weaknesses:

1. It can lead to embarrassment.
2. It can create a fear-driven foreign policy.

Embarrassment

The most recent example of this is in Afghanistan. Initially, the US supported Pakistan and its allies – notably the Taliban –

within Afghanistan, in opposition to Moscow's allies in the northern part of the country. Pakistan and the US didn't want their 'enemy' to gain control over the country. Since September 11, however, the US has changed sides and is now working with its former enemies against the Taliban to defeat Osama bin Laden.

In 1979, the Shah of Iran – a firm US ally – was driven from power by conservative clerics who regarded the US as the 'Great Satan'. In Iraq, Saddam Hussein decided to exploit the chaos in post-Shah Iran by invading the country in 1980. The Iran–Iraq war was one of the twentieth century's longest conflicts, and during its eight years the US helped to arm Iraq against its enemy, Iran. Then, in August 1990, Saddam Hussein suddenly invaded Kuwait. This time the US objected and helped Kuwait: US troops found themselves fighting Iraqi personnel armed with US equipment. After the war, the United Nations sent inspection teams with US advisers into Iraq to check on its progress towards disarmament, because they often encountered US equipment and so needed US advice on its military significance.

Fear

The philosophy 'The enemy of my enemy is my friend' is based on being suspicious about the rest of the world and always thinking the worst of everyone else. The Cold War – one of the most expensive government projects in world history – is a good example of how countries can live in fear of each other. The arms race during the Cold War was often based not so much on the real military situation of the time, but on worst-case scenarios of what the other side might produce in the future. In effect, each government was racing against its own fears rather than its enemy's actual ability. This same process is now under way with President Bush's national missile defence system, whose implementation could lead to the erosion of nuclear arms control.

Here's an alternative statement: 'The strongest person in the world is the person who can make their enemy their friend.' The emphasis here is on living by hope not by fear. Americans as individuals are outgoing, hopeful people, but this quality is rarely manifested in US foreign policy.

A foreign policy based on this new approach would look at what unites countries rather than what divides them. We might see countries working together on protecting the environment – for instance, ratifying the Kyoto Protocol on climate change – on disarmament, or giving more foreign aid. The US currently gives the lowest level of foreign aid (as a percentage of gross national product) out of all the countries in the developed world: 0.10 per cent. The UN target – which is met by only four of the twenty-two developed countries – is 0.7 per cent GNP.

In military terms, you don't win hearts and minds by putting people in coffins. The US military should take a lesson from the US business community and ask 'How can we win friends and influence people?'

20

? What are rogue states?

The term 'rogue states' was invented by the US Government to describe countries that are unfriendly towards it: for example, countries that facilitate terrorism overseas (but always against the US). The list tends to vary a little, with some countries moving on and off it, but standard entries have included Cuba, Iran, Iraq, Libya, Syria, North Korea and Sudan. Not all other countries agree with that list, however. For example, Australia and almost all the other UN member-nations don't agree that Cuba is a rogue state and each year the UN General Assembly adopts by a very large majority a non-binding resolution calling on the US to end its unilateral sanctions against Cuba. Australian companies have ignored the US sanctions and have traded with Cuba.

Iraq is off the list now, because the US hopes it will become a functioning democracy and a model for other Arab countries and Iran. There are still concerns about Syria, Iran and North Korea. Syria has been accused of assisting some of the terrorists in Iraq; and Iran and North Korea are on the list because of their nuclear weapons programs.

Libya is an interesting case study of how a country can come off the rogue state list. To examine the reasons for its removal I shall look first at why Libya was on the list.

On 1 September 1969, Muammar Gaddafi and a group of young military officers overthrew the regime of the 79-year-old King Idris, who was overseas. No one was killed. The king didn't try to organise a counter-coup, and died in exile.

Gaddafi abolished the monarchy and established the Libyan Arab Republic. These changes were welcomed by most Libyans, who didn't like the king's corrupt and inefficient rule. Gaddafi was also one of the first Arab leaders in the Middle East to defy the traditional power brokers in the region: the US and Britain. He closed down the British and American military bases, which had been established there after World War II when the colony was freed from Italian control. The country received its independence in 1951, but the British and Americans retained the military bases, including the famous British base at Tobruk. Arab governments, which opposed the creation of Israel, had criticised King Idris for allowing the Americans and British to remain, so Gaddafi's quick decision to expel them made him popular throughout the Arab world. The last of the foreign troops had left by 30 June 1970.

Oil was discovered in Libya in April 1959. With only about 6 million people, Libya is potentially one of the richest Arab countries on a per capita basis. In July 1970,

Libya nationalised the oil industry and in October 1970 it expelled the Italian settlers who had occupied parts of the country since Italy acquired the colony in 1911. Their land was shared out among the Libyans.

Within two years, then, Gaddafi had reorganised the country's internal affairs. Now he was set for the next stage: sponsoring international terrorism. Throughout the 1970s and 1980s, Gaddafi was well known for his support of terrorist organisations, which made the small country of Libya an unexpectedly powerful force in the world. Libya also provided refuge to Palestinian terrorist Abu Nidal, who was wanted in Israel and elsewhere for his terrorist activities.

In April 1984, Britain suspected that Libyan embassy officials were involved in shooting dead policewoman Yvonne Fletcher, who was patrolling outside the embassy in London. Libya was also suspected of supporting the Irish Republican Army (IRA), and so Britain severed its diplomatic relations with Libya.

Relations between the US and Libya also deteriorated. In May 1985, the US expelled all the employees of the Libyan People's Bureau (the embassy) in Washington DC for suspicious activities.

In March and April 1986, the US carried out a number of military attacks on Libya to assert its right to fly and sail near the Libyan coast. On 5 April there was a bomb attack on La Belle discotheque in West Berlin, in which two US servicemen and a Turkish woman were killed and 229 others were wounded. The US retaliated with a bombing raid on Libya on 15 April in which thirty-seven people were killed.

On 21 December 1988, a Pan Am Boeing 747 was blown up over the Scottish village of Lockerbie. British and American intelligence officials believed that Libyan agents were responsible for planting the bomb. In April 1990, British investigators announced that they had found an electronic component that linked two Libyan agents to the explosion. Throughout the 1990s, Libya refused to hand the agents over for an international trial. The United Nations imposed economic sanctions on Libya and it became isolated from most of the rest of the world.

In March 1989, Libyan agents blew up a French UTA plane over Niger, killing 170 people including the wife of the US ambassador to Chad.

The US Government has now decided Libya is no longer a rogue state, saying that it hasn't been involved in any foreign terrorism since 1994. Why has Libya changed its ways?

The most obvious explanation is that all of its expenditure on terrorism hasn't achieved a single military or political objective. The US and the UK didn't give in to terrorism, Israel still survives and the IRA hasn't won. Gaddafi opposed the 1979 peace treaty between Egypt and Israel yet it remains in effect. In November 1979, he financed the terrorist group that briefly took over the Great Mosque in Mecca. The Saudi royal family regained control of the mosque and remain in control of their country.

Gaddafi has given up on Arab leaders and has reduced his interest in Middle Eastern affairs. He now prefers to think of himself as an African leader, and wears African clothes as often as Arab ones.

Gaddafi doesn't like the rise of Islamic fundamentalism and he was one of the first leaders to warn the world about Osama bin Laden. In 1996 he was the target of an assassination attempt by the Libyan Islamic Fighting Group, sponsored by Osama bin Laden. On 11 September 2001, Gaddafi was one of the first leaders to express his condolences to President Bush for the acts of terrorism in the US.

A second reason is that the UN's economic sanctions hurt the country. Libya needs international markets, investment and expertise to get its oil industry moving again. Gaddafi has therefore disowned his terrorist past. In 1999 he handed over the two Libyan agents wanted in connection with the Lockerbie bombing. They were tried under Scottish law in a special court based in the Netherlands: one was found guilty and the other not guilty. Libya has paid an undisclosed amount of compensation to the next of kin of those killed in the bombing. Libya has also paid US$170 million to the next of kin of victims on the French UTA flight. Palestinian terrorist Abu Nidal was expelled in 1997, after being sheltered by Libya for a decade; and in 1999, Libya accepted 'general responsibility' for the murder of police constable Yvonne Fletcher and paid an unknown sum to her family.

In December 2003, Gaddafi renounced Libya's attempts to acquire weapons of mass destruction and invited international inspectors to check that Libya was no longer developing such weapons. This inspection enabled the west to learn a lot about AQ Khan's secret export of nuclear material from Pakistan.

The sanctions have been lifted against Libya: western companies are trading once more with the oil-rich country and Libya is now part of the international community again. On 24 March 2004, British Prime Minister Tony Blair visited Libya. This was the first time a British prime minister had been in the country since Churchill was there during World War II, and a clear sign that Gaddafi has at last come in from the cold.

Libya's case is proof that terrorism doesn't always work; Libya discovered that it can do better from international trade than from international terrorism.

21

? **Is the Russian empire likely to break up?**

Russia is highly unstable. The early 1990s saw the collapse of the Soviet empire in Eastern Europe. President Putin wants to hold his country together, but he has one of the world's most difficult jobs.

Geography works against Russia. The total length of the Russian empire covers ten time zones, stretching almost halfway across the globe. Moscow is actually closer to New York than it is to Vladivostok, and the Russians feel vulnerable about their Asian rear end.

Siberia and its Far East region have become Russia's new frontier, the area it most wants to develop. Siberia floats on an ocean of gas; the natural gas fields there are the world's largest. The region is also a treasure trove of other raw materials: Siberia produces 60 per cent of the country's timber, 60 per cent of its coal, and 80 per cent of its water. In Russia, gas is called 'blue gold', fur is 'soft gold', coal is 'black gold' and salmon is 'red gold'.

But Russia isn't technologically advanced enough to get at this wealth by its own means. For example, the ground in Siberia is frozen 300 metres deep for most of the year; it's as hard as concrete. Building foundations can only be installed by thawing the ground by steam, inserting the foundations and letting the ground refreeze. Gravedigging is impossible and so cremation is the only way to dispose of bodies. Russia needs foreign investment and expertise to cope with all these mining and drilling challenges, but foreign investors are reluctant to pour money into Russia because it is perceived as unstable.

This instability has two main causes:

1. The influence of the Russian Mafia.
2. The campaign in Chechnya for independence.

The influence of the Russian Mafia

Russian criminal gangs are among the most efficient and most brutal in the world. The Russian Mafia are a legacy from hundreds of years of tsarist rule followed by a Communist dictatorship. Daily existence was brutal under the tsars; violence was a way of life. The tsar who commissioned the building of the magnificent church on Moscow's Red Square, for example, ordered that all those who had worked on it must be blinded – he didn't want them going off to build a replica for another ruler. With the tsars treating their subjects badly, it's hardly surprising the subjects had few problems stealing from their rulers. They had to simply to survive.

Some Russians now romanticise the tsarist reign, but in 1917 the regime fell quickly partly because it was so deeply hated by many Russians. Later, under the Soviet system, theft became a way of life. The Soviet regime could put a man into space but it couldn't put goods on shop shelves, and so theft was a way of coping with government rationing. A criminal culture developed out of people's need to survive.

A central committee in Moscow decided how many items should be produced each year. In simplistic terms if the committee guessed correctly, then the consumers would be all right. But if the committee got it wrong, there was a shortage of those goods and so a black market developed. Peasants stole the food they grew, factory workers stole the products they made, doctors stole medicines and drivers stole petrol. All these items were sold on the black market and provided workers with an additional source of income.

The culture of crime ran through all levels of the system. Managers employed 'phantom' workers to receive additional salaries, or would label some of their goods as defective as a way of retaining them for sale on the black market. Goods that did get to retail shops were set aside for customers who would be willing to pay extra for them. Workers and managers were in on the schemes and pocketed some of the money. It was the normal way of life.

In Australia and other western countries, the black market caters to illegal tastes, such as drugs or weapons. In the Soviet Union, however, the items on the black market were ordinary goods that could be obtained no other way. In the Cold War days, Australian tourists travelling behind the Iron Curtain were advised to take gifts of coffee and jeans – items we took for granted but which were often not available to Russians because the central committee had guessed wrongly or – as in the case of jeans – didn't approve of them.

Workers often produced deliberately shoddy work, saying that the state pretended to pay them and so they pretended to work. If you wanted something done properly, they would oblige, but in their own time and at a price. Party officials at the top were also on the take. They expected bribes in exchange for their support. In short, there was no rule of law in the Soviet Union; no one had confidence in an honest legal system or an honest police force.

The only thing that made the streets of Moscow safe – especially for foreign tourists – was the presence of a network of spies. Bribery and theft at work were easy crimes to commit, because everyone else was on the take too. But very few premeditated murders were committed because of the network of neighbourhood spies – a person could not be sure that they would get away with a deliberate murder. The extensive system of mutual surveillance deterred murder. Instead, most non-government-sanctioned murders in the Communist era were done in a drunken haze in a domestic situation or a drinking session among erstwhile friends. Many of the murders were actually reported to the police by the murderer. Meanwhile, there was no scrutiny of what was going on in the Soviet Union. There were no free media, so it was no good complaining to a newspaper or radio or television program. No one would take up your case if it was likely to cause some embarrassment to the system.

The Soviet Union was collapsing from the inside. When Mikhail Gorbachev became the Soviet leader in 1985 he thought he could reform the system. In fact, it was far too rotten to be saved. As soon as Gorbachev started making changes, the entire structure fell like a house of playing cards. The Soviet Union finally collapsed in 1991, but its criminal culture had already provided the foundations and training ground for the Russian Mafia. Generations of Russians had been educated in this criminal culture and so the gangs had plenty of potential recruits, people who knew from hard experience what they had to do to survive.

As the Soviet empire in Eastern Europe collapsed, the troops were brought home and demobilised. There were no government plans for how these soldiers could enter civilian life; they just walked off their bases with as much military equipment as they could carry. Many joined the Russian Mafia, and the gangs are therefore well armed and their members well trained.

Protection rackets have become a way of life. Businesspeople are warned that they need to pay some money to avoid their premises suddenly catching fire or being destroyed in other ways. The Mafia are also able to make use of globalisation now that Russia is friendly with western countries. Russian citizens can move easily in and out of western countries on legitimate visas. They can also open bank accounts in other countries and hide their money overseas as legitimate customers.

The poor are having a bad time in Russia. The reorganisation of the country has been extremely badly handled and the government's assets have been 'privatised', which has increased the gulf between the very rich and the very poor. We might ask how it was possible to privatise property when the country had no tradition of property rights. Consequently, the poor have lost out on all opportunities – legal and illegal – to make money. Russia is the only developed country in world history to have a declining life expectancy and therefore a declining population. Life has become so grim there that Russians are dying at a rate of about half a million people per year. At this rate, it will be empty in a century or so.

Meanwhile, life there has become far more dangerous. The murder rate in Moscow is now three or four times higher than that of New York City. Journalists reporting on crime become targets themselves; they die for their honesty.

The Mafia enjoy close links with the country's ruling elite – the fox now guards the chickens. And there are fears that, having done so well in Russia, the Mafia are looking for more opportunities overseas. Russian mobsters currently operate in about fifty countries around the world. The Australian Government is concerned that they are trying to expand their links here too.

The campaign in Chechnya for independence

Chechnya is Russia's biggest terrorist problem. The Chechens, numbering about a million, are mainly Sunni Muslims who have always disliked the Orthodox Christians and then the Communists who have run Russia. They claim that they've never fully accepted Russian rule and whenever Russia is in trouble, the Chechens take the opportunity to try to re-establish independence. Moscow can't withdraw from that republic and yet there is no easy way of winning the war. Thousands of people have been killed – on a per capita basis, this is one of the world's most violent wars currently under way – and many more will die before a political settlement is reached.

The first wave of Russian rule was 1818–1917. The Russian Empire gradually expanded from the northeast corner of present-day Russia to all parts of the world's largest landmass. Unlike the British or French empires, which required large navies, the Russians simply expanded like an inkblot on paper, rolling out over the land. Russian rule went south and reached the North Caucasus in the late eighteenth century, but was resisted by local Muslim warlords, who wanted to run their own affairs along Islamic lines.

Russia controlled the region from 1858, when it defeated Imam Shamil's rebellion. Russia was determined to win, because the region provided the potential for another route into the Middle East and eventually the Mediterranean, but the victory came only after much suffering and the commitment of many military resources to the struggle.

The first wave of Russian rule ended in 1917 with the communist revolution and the collapse of the tsarist rule. The Russian empire fell into chaos and the Chechens made a declaration of independence. The independence didn't last long: when the Russian civil war finished, the Communists established their rule over Chechnya in 1924.

The next window of opportunity came after Hitler's invasion of the Soviet Union in June 1941. Some Chechens collaborated with the advancing Nazis in the hope that Hitler would give them independence. But in 1944 Hitler was driven out of the Caucasus region and Stalin punished the Chechens for their disloyalty with a mass deportation of 400,000–800,000 people to Siberia. About 100,000 perished during the deportation. When Stalin died in 1953, the surviving deportees were returned to Chechnya in 1956 and the republic of Chechnya was re-established in 1957.

This deportation episode helps explain why Chechen nationalism has been more radical, more violent and more anti-Russian than that of Russia's other Muslim ethnic minorities. There is a long history of hatred on both sides. The current Chechen fighting is particularly brutal. Other groups attempt to win sympathy from international public opinion by trying to be careful whom they target, but the Chechen terrorists hate the Russians and have no qualms about the brutality of their tactics. In recent years many ordinary civilians have been caught up in their fighting.

When Mikhail Gorbachev's economic and political reforms spun out of control and the Soviet Union fell apart in 1990–91, Chechens decided they would try once more for independence. At this time, Moscow's Eastern Europe empire (taken over after World War II) regained independence and so did the Islamic republics along the USSR's southern border between the Caspian Sea and China.

Russia's new President, Boris Yeltsin, refused Chechnya's declaration of independence but waited three years, until 1994, before sending in troops to quash the rebellion. Yeltsin's Defence Minister, Pavel Grachev, predicted the Chechen rebels would be put down in a matter of days. In 1996, the Russian troops were driven out, and a further attack on Chechnya took place in October 1999. The situation has remained violent since then.

In October 2002, Chechens took over a Moscow theatre and held 129 people hostage. Forty-one Chechen fighters were killed when Russian troops stormed the building. In December 2003, a female suicide bomber killed five people near Moscow's Red Square. In February 2004, a bomb attack killed thirty-nine people on the Moscow underground. In May 2004, the pro-Moscow Chechen President was killed in Grozny. On 24 August 2004, two planes were blown up soon after leaving Moscow airport. On 31 August 2004, a suicide bomber killed ten people in the forecourt of a Moscow underground station. The biggest attack was also the most recent: in September 2004 on the Beslan school in the neighbouring republic of North Ossetia.

Oil is now a major additional factor in the war. It is assumed the Caspian Sea will become a new 'Middle East' because of its vast oil reserves, and Chechnya is one of the republics straddling the land between the Black and Caspian Seas. A major oil pipeline carries oil from the western side of the Caspian Sea through Chechnya towards the Ukraine. Grozny, the republic's capital city, is – or was, before the recent fighting – an important oil-refining point. Although the republic had a population of only a million people and only a small oil reserve, it was very important in the grand scheme of oil politics.

There has been speculation that the next few years could see the collapse of the Russian empire. Politically, President Putin can't afford to give Chechnya independence. If this unruly republic is allowed to break away, then others will also do so. For example, some people in Siberia would also like to go their own way. Siberia has many resources and so could afford to be independent, but no leader wants to go into the history books as presiding over the dissolution of his or her country. Putin will fight to retain control over Chechnya as an example to other republics.

The US, from 1991 onwards, was very critical of Russia's great use of force against the Chechens, but President Putin may now receive some political assistance from the United States. On 11 September 2001, Putin was one of the first world leaders to contact President Bush to express his regret at the terrorist attacks in New York and Washington DC. He reminded Bush that the Americans were now experiencing what the Russians had long had to endure from the Chechens. Since September 11, Bush hasn't criticised Russian violence in Chechnya.

Meanwhile, Putin has been anxious to show how the Chechen fighters have been receiving assistance from people linked with Osama bin Laden. He regards Russia as being part of the front line in the War on Terrorism. Putin refuses to negotiate with Chechen terrorists. Indeed, there are so many different warlords that it's difficult to see just who does represent Chechen opinion. But it's also difficult to see how Russian violence alone will beat the terrorists.

Incidentally, the USSR didn't learn from the US's experience in Vietnam when it went into Afghanistan and lost the war there. Much the same could be said about Russia's campaign in Chechnya: the military claimed in December 1994 that it would be over in only a few days, but it dragged on for years and resulted only in a fragile truce.

Also, because this was Russia's first televised war, the troops had to be careful about their use of force. Old women sitting in front of Russian tanks made for effective opponents in this new era of transparency. In Stalin's day, the tanks would have run over the raging grannies, but with the mass media watching, this was no longer possible.

22

? Should Australia accept more refugees?

Yes. Australia accepts about 13,000 refugees per year – a tiny number by world standards. Total refugee numbers vary from one year to the next, from between about 12 million and 22 million people. Out of the seventy-one countries that accept refugees, Australia is ranked thirty-second. So Australia isn't being 'swamped' by refugees, and could do a lot more to welcome them.

Refugees and migrants

There are major differences between refugees and migrants. Refugees are forced to flee their country; they don't necessarily want to leave.

The basic 1951 Refugee Convention defines a 'refugee' as:

Any person who, owing to a well-founded fear of being persecuted for reasons of race, religion, nationality, membership of a particular social group or political opinion, is outside the country of his/her nationality and is unable, or owing to such fear, is unwilling to avail himself/herself of the protection of that country.

This is an international law matter and the focus is on the individual's needs.

By contrast, migrants make a conscious decision to go to a particular country; they want to leave their own country. About 110,000 migrants are allowed into Australia each year; about half are to help with the country's skill shortages and the other half are family reunions. Most migrants can return to their original home if they want to.

Migration law is a domestic matter. It depends upon what a national government may decide and the focus is on that country's needs.

Unfortunately, people often use the terms 'refugees' and 'migrants' interchangeably and so create an incorrect impression of the number of refugees entering Australia. In my experience with talkback radio programs, people frequently have an inflated idea of how many refugees are allowed into Australia each year.

Most refugees remain in the neighbouring country they've fled to. Many will return home in due course, usually after a change in the political circumstances. The two biggest sources of refugees in recent years have been Afghanistan and Iraq – and both now have undergone major political changes. At one point Pakistan had about 2.5 million Afghanis sheltering within its borders.

One value of the US intervention in both Afghanistan and Iraq, and the resulting increase in emergency relief, is that there has been less need for people to flee overseas and so the number of asylum seekers heading to Australia (and elsewhere) has declined significantly. This drop in asylum seekers has had nothing to do with the Howard Government's tough stand, which was more a domestic matter of responding to media hysteria and winning elections.

We've also heard asylum seekers being referred to as 'queue jumpers'. But there were no queues to jump in Saddam Hussein's Iraq or the Taliban's Afghanistan because the Australian Department of Immigration didn't have branch offices there. Australia didn't approve of those countries' policies and so relations were virtually non-existent.

Almost all of the asylum seekers from Iraq and Afghanistan were granted refugee status by the Howard Government.

'Illegals'

Under international law, there is no such thing as an 'illegal' asylum seeker. The people who wrote the original 1951 Refugee Convention knew about the real-life experiences of the Jews who fled Hitler. Sometimes people have to arrive in a country without official papers because their own government wouldn't allow them to leave. Therefore, people who arrive in Australia without proper documents or with false documents aren't 'illegal'. They're 'asylum seekers' – a term that is recognised under international law.

A real 'illegal' is a person who has overstayed their ordinary migration visa. The biggest offenders are young

British tourists, who fall in love with Australia during their one-year holiday visit and don't want to go home.

From Iron Curtain to Glass Curtain

The mass movement of people is nothing new. Throughout history wars have often forced people to leave their homes. In the 1970s, as many as 10 million people fled from what was then East Pakistan into India – the largest single human displacement in modern history. Pakistan fell apart and Bangladesh was eventually created from East Pakistan.

The basic international law of refugees reflects the bad conscience western countries felt over their treatment of the Jews in the 1930s. When Hitler came to power in 1933, he started violating Jewish human rights. Western countries didn't let Jewish refugees enter their countries, as we've seen in the section 'Will there ever be peace in Israel and Palestine?', and many Jews who were trapped in the Nazi area were killed there.

After World War II, the west thought it was necessary to do more for future refugees. The 1948 Universal Declaration of Human Rights (which Australia helped to write) stated in Article 14: 'Everyone has the right to seek and to enjoy in other countries asylum from persecution'.

During the Cold War, western countries welcomed the refugees from Communism. In the early 1980s on a trip to West Berlin, President Reagan challenged the Soviets to tear down the Iron Curtain that ran north–south through Germany and the city of Berlin. In 1989, peace activists did just that.

Nowadays, western governments have erected a Glass Curtain. Thanks to the media revolution, people in poorer countries know what life is like in the west. But, having encouraged a greater sense of freedom, western countries now want to keep people out.

The best way to keep people at home is to give them more of an incentive to stay there. Most refugees don't want to flee anyway. Leaving their homeland means they lose contact with friends and relatives, and they may not be able to speak English. Therefore, we need to be careful about which governments we support overseas, and we should give more foreign aid to assist development prospects.

Would terrorists pose as refugees as a way of entering Australia?

This would be most unlikely. Australia is a very difficult country to enter. It's surrounded by water and much of the coastline is rugged and inhospitable. It's also some distance from any other country. Besides, entering Australia as a refugee would automatically give that person some kind of official record. They would be known to the authorities right from the outset.

Basic intelligence tradecraft suggests that a terrorist would enter Australia on a legitimate business – or possibly educational – visa. The person would stay at a good hotel, not make any terrorist mission-related calls from the hotel telephone (they would use different public telephones some distance from the hotel) and avoid taking taxis from the rank outside the hotel. They wouldn't leave bottles or drug syringes in their hotel wastepaper baskets, wouldn't try to get call girls into their hotel rooms and would avoid being ostentatious consumers or tippers. In short, they wouldn't do anything to draw attention to themselves. Later, when the police are investigating the terrorist attack, hotel staff would be unlikely to remember much about the 'normal' and 'respectable' guest.

All the September 11 terrorists entered the US legally, either as students, tourists or business visitors.

Looming skills shortage

Australia needs more people for economic reasons. Australians haven't been having enough babies to replenish the population and there's a looming skill shortage. It's already obvious in professions requiring more young adults, such as teachers, nurses and defence personnel. Despite what racist politicians may say, Australia will need to accept more people – or confront economic decline.

One indicator of potential economic growth is the arrival of people from overseas. Refugees and migrants are survivors; they're inventive and want to make a better life. Both can help Australia's economic growth – as indeed they did in the post-war period after 1945.

A 2005 edition of the magazine *Refugees*, published by the UN High Commission for Refugees, reported extensively on the remarkable story of Utica in upstate New York. The town used to be a jewel in the US's industrial era, but became a case study of its industrial decline. The factories were closed down, the jobs moved elsewhere and the town's population fell from 120,000 to 65,000 today.

Now, however, the town is a case study of how refugees can revive a region. Americans welcomed refugees from some of the worst places in the world, including Vietnam, Myanmar (Burma), Somalia and the former Soviet Union. About 10,000 people are refugees. The town's Republican mayor, Tim Julian, has credited the town's revival to the arrival of the refugees, describing how their energy, their thirst to make a better life, their survival skills and the skills acquired in their homelands have all played a part. Despite September 11 and the fears from the War on Terrorism, Mayor Julian looks forward to welcoming still more refugees.

Here is a lesson for Australia.

23

❓ What is microcredit and how is it changing the lives of women in Bangladesh?

The poor of the world don't lack initiative or motivation; they lack credit. They're often caught in a debt trap to moneylenders and middle people. If they can borrow small sums of money from reputable sources they can create their own businesses and work their way out of poverty.

'Microcredit' consists of tiny collateral-free loans aimed at the poorest of the poor to help them start or expand self-employment pursuits. It's a very good way of giving foreign aid. Foreign aid is a comparatively new idea. In previous centuries, colonies were created to supply money to the imperial powers, rather than the imperial powers giving money to the colonies. Imperial powers went in search of lands and people they could exploit as colonies.

Then, in the 1940s, General George Marshall, the US Secretary of State, proposed that the US supply about 2 per cent of its gross national product (GNP) to assist post-war reconstruction in Europe. The program was called the Marshall Plan and remains the largest percentage figure ever given to foreign aid by any country. It was one of the US's greatest achievements in its history and a great success – but also a misleading one. To this day it is fashionable for people to call for a new 'Marshall Plan' to help countries rebuild after a war (as in Iraq) or a natural catastrophe (like the December 2004 Asian tsunami). But when the colonies became independent and the UN's first Development Decade was proclaimed in the 1960s, we overestimated what could be achieved by foreign aid in developing countries. Europe in the 1940s and '50s had an educated workforce, an existing – if badly damaged – infrastructure and potential markets. By contrast, developing countries often lack those basic advantages.

In more recent years, governments in developed countries have used their foreign aid for the benefit of their own companies. Nowadays, most foreign aid is 'tied': that is, the receiving country is limited as to where and how the money can be spent. In fact, most of Australia's foreign aid never actually leaves Australia. For example, I taught a course on the politics of international aid at the University of New South Wales in Sydney. Some of the overseas students were financed by Australia's overseas aid program; therefore the university was a recipient of some foreign aid.

After about fifty years of international foreign aid, there are continuing concerns about poverty in developing countries and a recognition that traditional foreign aid is not working. Besides, foreign aid is drying up. Australia now gives the lowest level on record. The UN target is 0.7 per cent of GNP; Australia gives around 0.29 per cent. The US, which gave 2 per cent during the Marshall Plan era, now gives only 0.1 per cent, most of which goes to Israel and Egypt.

Microcredit shifts the focus off charity and on to self-reliance. In Bangladesh, for example, the Christian World Service – a program of the National Council of Churches in Australia (to which all the mainstream churches belong) – is cooperating with the Christian Commission for Development in Bangladesh (CCDB) to establish a microcredit program. People with very little money can apply for a small interest-free loan, which they can use to start their own business. They then repay the loan through the proceeds of the business. Once the loan is paid off, they completely own their own business, guaranteeing an income for the future. And their repayments to CCDB are used to provide someone else with the chance to start a new business.

Chena is one Bangladeshi case study. Chena used her microcredit loan to buy a dozen chickens, plus a cage to keep them in. Now she sells up to 400 chickens a day at market, and has an additional 200 laying eggs. She's been able to purchase a mobile phone so she can call the markets to find out the prices before she takes the chickens in; this way she won't undersell them.

Now Chena is helping another woman to start her own business by allowing her access to her cart. She's paid back the loan in full and owns her own brick home with electricity, a fridge, a fan and a fluorescent light – all very rare possessions in Bangladesh. Chena's entrepreneurial skills are a step forward for the new role of women in her country.

Microcredit is an economic 'third way': it helps the poorest of the poor and it encourages people to become self-reliant entrepreneurs. It makes use of the free market to help people and reduces the need for government intervention in the economy. Microcredit is a hand-up, not a hand-out. It should be encouraged by both ends of the Australian political spectrum.

24

❓ Is the world running out of oil?

Yes, the world is running out of oil, but we still have some time to go, although there's little agreement on just how much time that might be.

There's a difference between actually running out of oil and no longer finding oil at the same rate that it's being drilled. Think of it like getting apples off a tree – there may be apples right at the top of the tree, but would you want to make all the effort to get there? Similarly, there will always be some oil left on the earth, but the last drops will be too expensive and too difficult to get out of the ground.

Oil experts call this issue the 'Huppert Peak': oil production reaches a peak, where about half the supply of the find is used, after which it becomes increasingly difficult and expensive to extract the other half. The name comes from M. King Huppert, a Shell geologist, who in 1956 predicted that US oil production would peak around 1970 (he was proved right) and global output would peak in 1995 (he got that wrong). (For more information on this, see: http://www.peakoil.net.)

The basic question is: has most of the world's oil been found or are companies just not working hard enough to locate and drill? When does the world reach the Huppert Peak?

We can't know fully what's happening with the world oil situation, because some countries – the Middle East and Russia, for example – control foreign involvement in their industry and so we don't have access to all the information. It might be that these oil suppliers exaggerate their reserves so as to discourage other countries from working harder on developing alternative energy sources, such as solar or nuclear power. Are they playing a game of cat and mouse to lull us into a false sense of security about oil?

We do know there have been no major oil finds in recent years. The biggest recent find – a field in Kazakhstan in 2000 – will only produce enough oil to last the world four months. On the other hand, the technology of exploration has improved considerably and so that side of the industry is more efficient. If oil prices rise, this will focus greater attention on finding new fields. Meanwhile, new countries are being opened up for oil exploration – for example, in the vast Central Asia region formerly controlled by the USSR: Azerbaijan, Kazakhstan and Turkmenistan. The Caspian Sea region is becoming almost a new 'Middle East' in terms of all the oil-exploration activities.

Where there is much more agreement is on the fact that oil is a 'strategic commodity'. Future historians will call this era the 'Age of Oil'. Modern economies are based on oil, not just to power cars, but for a range of other products such as fertiliser, DVDs, rubber, cheap air flights, plastics and metals.

Oil meets 40 per cent of the world's energy needs and nearly 90 per cent of its transportation needs. Military forces run on oil. When Winston Churchill converted the Royal Navy from coal-burning to oil-burning almost a century ago, he transformed the world's greatest navy, giving it greater speed and mobility. It is now impossible to imagine the world's defence forces without oil; the world's largest single user of oil is the US defence force.

In trading terms, oil is also unusual. Oil stocks can be manipulated in a way that other commodities cannot be. Foodstuffs go off and so cannot be stockpiled; other commodities can be substituted for similar ones – such as tea for coffee; but oil is unique. And there may be many other potential suppliers of the other commodities, while there are few major suppliers of oil.

In 1973, the dramatic decision by the members of the Organization of Petroleum Exporting Countries (OPEC) to increase the price of oil was a turning point in world affairs. Arab countries had attacked Israel and to deter western countries from coming to Israel's aid, the OPEC countries cut off the supply of oil to them. When the war ended (in another Israeli victory), they increased the price of oil and have since maintained a high price for it. This price increase changed a great deal. It gave Arab countries and Iran more control over their economies; it greatly increased their national pride, because for the first time in centuries they were dominating western countries; and it gave them vastly increased wealth.

There was even speculation that the oil price rise could cause the end of the western financial system, with the oil dollars piling up in the OPEC countries. It was said that the west's post-World War II economic boom came to an end in 1973 with westerners standing forlornly in a queue waiting for petrol. But the world's financial system managed to survive that crisis and many people forgot the fears generated in 1973 until the increasing debate over the Huppert Peak revived them.

Increasing global demand

The US remains the number one consumer of oil but is no longer the number one producer; instead, it's now the number one importer. Motorists consume nearly half the daily supply of oil. The US is choosing to ignore the potential problems of supply and isn't making contingency plans such as paying more attention to public transport and the better design of cities. American consumers are reluctant to apply conservation methods, and there is no political leadership to do so. President Bush could have used the sense of urgency from the September 11 terrorist attack to convince Americans to take oil conservation more seriously, for example.

China is now the number two consumer of oil, taking over what was previously Japan's position. The dramatic growth of the Chinese economy makes it difficult to predict global oil demand. Meanwhile, India and other Asian countries are also growing rapidly. Given the significance of oil for modern economies, a crisis or panic in the oil industry will flow through to the rest of the world.

Another concern is that the suppliers are not necessarily stable regimes. The US has sought a primary role in Middle East oil since the early 1930s – and it can't afford to change now. Some people have argued that the need to control oil was the motivator for the US's 2003 invasion of Iraq. The US's involvement in Afghanistan in 2001 may also have been motivated by the desire to secure western Afghanistan as a route for oil pipelines running south from the Central Asian oil fields through Pakistan and out to the Indian Ocean (currently they head north into Russia).

The US speculated about invading Saudi Arabia in 1973 at the time of the OPEC crisis. Today, Saudi Arabia is on Osama bin Laden's hit list: he wants to overthrow the House of Saud. Given the risks to the Saudi regime and its fragility, might we see the US speculating once more about how best to protect its interests in the oil fields?

Meanwhile China also wants more oil and is working on improving relations with Arab countries in the Middle East and Iran. For example, China is opposed to US-led sanctions on Iran over its nuclear weapons program. Iran also wants to stay on good terms with China. The fundamentalist Muslims who run Iran admire the ability of the Chinese Communists to encourage economic change without political change. That is also their aim and so they are willing to learn from the Communists how to do it. Money talks all languages.

China is taking the quest for oil right up to the US borders, encouraging Canada to build east–west pipelines to transport oil to the Pacific coast, where it can be taken by ship to China, instead of just north–south down into the US. China's oil ambitions also have implications for the US military. The US military is the world's largest single user of oil, but China (and the other rapidly expanding economies) are becoming competitors for that oil. Will China be able to ground the US defence forces?

Meanwhile, there are fears that terrorists will target the sea lanes carrying oil tankers. There's also the risk of a suicide air attack, such as on Saudi Arabia's Abqaiq complex, the world's largest oil refinery near the Persian Gulf.

In late 2004, there were reports that Margaret Thatcher's son, Mark, then based in South Africa, was implicated in an attempted coup in an obscure west African country. He was cleared of being involved, but the question arose of why foreigners would want to get involved in trying to take over a west African country. The answer is oil. Keep an eye on what's going on in west Africa – such as military coups – because the value of the offshore oil fields along their coasts is increasing rapidly. The US overall now relies more on African oil than Saudi oil. African nations may not have the same large reserves as the Middle East or the Caspian Sea, but every drop counts.

As the world's easily available oil is extracted, it becomes necessary to find other locations. These may be in obscure countries with harsh terrains and governments who are anti-western, but the world is addicted to oil and so we have no choice but to negotiate with such countries.

Two unstable oil-supplying countries

A large concern about the future of global oil supplies is the instability of the regimes in the supplying countries.

Saudi Arabia has about 25 per cent of the world's proven oil reserves and the oil is easy to obtain. The Ghawar field was discovered in 1948 and is still the largest oil field ever found. Saudi Arabia therefore plays a key role in moderating the international price: it can flood the market during oil shortages with a new supply and so prevent others from pushing up the price.

The Saudi regime manages to knit together traditional tribal clan structures and very conservative Wahhabi Islamic clerics. The country was formed in 1932 when tribal leader Abdul Aziz ibn Saud took control over much of the Arabian peninsula and named the country in his tribe's honour. There is no democracy in Saudi Arabia: citizens don't pay tax and so the ruling elite feel no obligation to be accountable to them. Although it's one of the world's driest countries, water is almost free; there's also free education, health and business loans for its own citizens. But living in paradise can become tedious and many young Saudis are bored and aimless.

The ruling regime consists of about 50,000 people. There's some doubt about the exact size of the elite, because some of the men – who have more than one wife – aren't sure exactly how many children they have. Osama bin Laden, for example, whose billionaire father is part of that elite, has about fifty brothers and sisters. The 50,000 elite govern a population of 22 million, of whom 16 million are Saudi. The country relies on many migrant workers (who generally lead a tougher life) to do the menial tasks – it's not a paradise for them.

A big problem for the regime is that Saudi income is lower now than it was thirty years ago. The boom years are over and there's little to show for the post-1973 oil revenue; much of the money has been squandered on foreign military equipment and projects of dubious wealth. Meanwhile, people in their twenties and thirties have few opportunities. Out of the nineteen September 11 terrorists, fifteen were wealthy, educated young Saudi men, who looked to Osama bin Laden to provide their lives with a sense of meaning.

There's a huge contradiction in Saudi life. On the one hand, the society is wealthy and therefore open to new technology and new ideas from overseas; citizens are also able to travel overseas. On the other hand, citizens are subject to extensive daily governmental and religious control and so are unable to make much of this beneficial impact of globalisation.

It's very difficult to get inside information on the country. Foreigners have limited scope for internal travel, unless they are Muslim. Those foreigners who may hear information about the fragility of the cheap oil supply – for example, foreign contractors such as building or engineering companies – won't speak about it for fear of risking their contracts. How will future historians treat us for relying on such a small, fragile regime for so much of our wealth?

The situation is only a little better in Russia, which is now about the same size as Saudi Arabia in terms of oil production. Russia, as a capitalist country, is now trading oil on the international market; because it's outside OPEC it could be helpful in eroding OPEC's power. (OPEC accounted for 80 per cent of the world's traded oil in 1973, but now it is only 40 per cent.)

Unfortunately, the Russian oil industry is in turmoil as President Putin seeks to centralise control over his ramshackle country. Putin wants greater control over the oil industry, and his government has enforced bankruptcy on Russia's main oil producer, the Yukos corporation, because he feared it was becoming too influential in Russian politics.

The Russian political situation remains unstable overall. Russia is the world's largest landmass and it's difficult for Moscow to hold the various ethnic groups together. Additionally, Russia is still having difficulty converting the Communist economy to a capitalist one. Foreign oil corporations have no ethical problems about the types of leaders they deal with – they happily do business with corrupt and brutal Arab regimes – but they do need stability of supply, and that stability is under threat in Russia.

25

❓ Is the world running out of water?

The freshwater crisis is far more severe than many other environmental issues that receive more media attention, such as climate change. Water is the single most precious element for life on earth. It is probably the only natural resource to touch all aspects of human civilisation, and there is no alternative to it. We can't diversify away from it. Water is hard-wired, so to speak, into agriculture, industry and culture.

The entire population of the world lives on the 2.5 per cent of the planet's water that is both fresh and accessible. The largest reserve of freshwater is the Antarctic ice shelf, which contains about 80 per cent of the world's supply of freshwater.

In Australia, we all know about the shortage of our freshwater supplies. Australia is the world's oldest, flattest and driest continent. Indigenous peoples made a success of living lightly upon the land for around 100,000 years and managed to survive all the different climatic conditions. But the more recent European agriculture and lifestyles may not be compatible with Australia's environment. For example, the destruction of trees for land clearing has caused problems with salination. Additionally, there has not been enough financial incentive to use water wisely.

Australia isn't the only country with freshwater problems. In the Middle East, water shortages have the potential to cause wars. The US is currently mediating between Israel and Lebanon over the Hasbani River, the main water artery in the region. Also, Israel and Jordan are trying to save the Dead Sea (whose level is falling by about a metre a year) – this is their biggest cooperation agreement since 1994.

Israel is a pioneer in the field of water conservation. For example, instead of scattering water on leaves (where it may evaporate), it drip feeds smaller amounts of water direct to roots and stems. But Israel still has a serious water problem. Its water comes from three main sources: the Sea of Galilee and two aquifers (underground supplies). One aquifer runs down the coast of Israel and the second begins in the territory of the West Bank before flowing underground into Israel itself. The Palestinians, with their high population growth rate, have even less water.

A possible solution would involve one or two water pipes that would transfer water from eastern Turkey's Seyhan and Ceyhan rivers across to the Middle East and provide water for all the countries of the region. These pipelines would also benefit eastern Turkey, bringing money into the poor regions that are water-rich. Unfortunately, international politics – for the moment anyway – rules out such an obvious solution.

No single measure would do more to reduce disease and save lives in the developing world than bringing safe water and adequate sanitation to all. Ninety per cent of the diseases of the world are water-related. Globally, one in two hospital beds is occupied by a person suffering from water-borne diseases.

So how can we address the world's freshwater crisis?

First of all, countries need to rethink their agricultural practices. Agriculture is the main user of water, especially irrigation. Australian farmers, in particular, rely on irrigation, and the irrigation lobby is very powerful. But perhaps it's time to accept that these European-style practices aren't as successful in Australia.

Another option is the conversion of saltwater into freshwater, whether by distillation or filtering through a membrane. This is an energy-intensive process, though there may be scope for developing new solar energy industries to power such conversion, not least in Australia. Instead of trying to turn rivers inland, we ought to be focusing on new ways of financing solar energy research. It is bizarre that Australia, a country that receives so much sunlight, should be so slow to find ways of generating solar energy.

Finally, we need to reconsider our approach to the cost of water. Some economists complain that the conversion of saltwater into freshwater is too expensive, but perhaps the real problem lies in the pricing policy for water. The issue is not one of whether the water supply should be privatised, but that consumers should be paying a realistic price for their water – no matter who supplies it. If water is more expensive, people will be more careful in how they use it. An increase in the cost of water may also force the agricultural industries to reconsider their approach to water usage.

There are many more dead civilisations than currently flourishing ones and a key factor in their demise was the loss of water or food. It remains to be seen whether we can do better this time.

26

❓ Will the United States end up as just another tourist attraction?

No great power has remained one forever. Every country has risen and fallen. Will the US be next?

Great powers decline for many reasons: overextension of their lines of communication; the rise of even stronger rivals; exhaustion of natural resources; corruption. But there is always a common theme: arrogance. A country in decline is unable to diagnose it because it believes that it will remain powerful forever. Many of the statues of great people in London were built just as the world's greatest empire was beginning its slow decline. And few people in the early 1980s predicted such a dramatic collapse of the Soviet Union in the late 1980s. Great powers often fall faster than it took for them to become great in the first place.

Imperial overstretch

In 1987, Professor Paul Kennedy, a British historian now resident in the US, triggered a debate that continues today. In his best-selling book, *The Rise and Fall of the Great Powers*, he surveyed 500 years of European empires: Spain, Portugal, the Netherlands, France, Germany and Britain. He detected a similar pattern: each began as a small trading country, then acquired overseas trade links, then developed a strong military to protect its trade interests, then got involved in foreign wars, and then went into decline. Each started out small and efficient, but became large, overly ambitious and suffered from what he called 'imperial overstretch' – they acquired too many foreign commitments and tried to do too many things.

I've added my own final stage to the Kennedy cycle: the great power finally ends up as a tourist attraction. Spain, Portugal and the Netherlands were mighty powers in their day, but today they are visited mainly by sightseers.

Kennedy warned Americans to be careful, because it seemed to him that the US was following that same cycle.

Until the Japanese attack on Pearl Harbor on 7 December 1941, the US was not a major military power. The country's first president, George Washington, advised against getting involved in foreign alliances, and isolationism remains a strong theme in US history. (Eighty per cent of members of Congress don't have passports.) Despite President Washington's warning, the US has turned itself into the international police officer. It's involved in major military operations in the Balkans, Afghanistan and Iraq and elsewhere.

Kennedy's theory has been rejected by some American commentators. They argue that it is possible to learn from history and so countries are not doomed to follow the same depressing cycle. The US economy can afford small wars, and besides, the US does well not only in 'hard' (military) power but also in 'soft' power, such as entertainment and consumer tastes. Hollywood still makes the best dreams. The US also wins the international 'war for talent' because skilled people want to live there (including Australian scientists) and so it's able to constantly develop its technological skills. Finally, national security is now based less on territory and natural resources and more on the ability to integrate into the global economy – and most transnational corporations are American.

There is now a more explicit debate in the US over the US 'empire', however. Some critics claim that the US began its imperial career a century ago, with the war on the Spanish (out of which it acquired Guantanamo Base on Cuba), and are concerned about imperial overstretch.

In the 2000 presidential election, for example, Governor George Bush promised that he wouldn't do any 'nation-building', unlike President Clinton had done in places like Bosnia in the Balkans. The US, Bush said, didn't have the skill or resources for that type of work. But since 11 September 2001, this is exactly what President Bush has been doing in Afghanistan and Iraq. The work has been carried out without much success but at a great cost.

The limitations of military power

A country isn't rich *because* it has a large military force; it has a large military force because it is rich and so can afford it. The US is now the world's only superpower. It has the nuclear capacity to destroy all of the world's population several times over and accounts for more than a third of the world's total military expenditure. The US spends five times more than second-place Japan; indeed, it spends more than the next eight biggest spenders combined. But is all that money well spent? Does power still come from the barrel of the gun? There are at least five negative responses to that question.

First, the US has been unsuccessful against guerrilla groups, most notably in Vietnam. It is still bogged down in Afghanistan and Iraq.

Second, the US has had little success against some long-running irritants. Take Cuba, for instance. When Fidel Castro, Che Guevara and their party of eighty-two landed in Cuba in December 1956, Cuban President Batista and US President Eisenhower didn't take them very seriously. All but twelve were quickly mopped up and the survivors fled to the hills in Sierra Maestra. But within three years, their guerrilla struggle had brought them to power. President Castro is now celebrating almost fifty years of running Cuba and is one of the world's longest-serving heads of state. He's beaten the ten US presidents who tried to defeat him. The US has maintained economic sanctions against Cuba for forty years. As I've mentioned in 'What are rogue states?', each year the United Nations General Assembly adopts a non-binding resolution calling on the US to end sanctions, and only Israel and Uzbekistan now support the US policy.

Third, having nuclear weapons is no guarantee of military victory. The limitation of nuclear weapons arises from their extensive capacity to kill: they're too destructive to use in regular military campaigns. Nuclear weapons destroy that which the attacker would like eventually to control. Even though the UK had nuclear weapons, this didn't deter Argentina from invading the Falklands in 1982.

Additionally, nuclear missiles can't be shot down. Even if President Reagan's Strategic Defence Initiative ('star wars') had gone ahead and developed the means to shoot down some missiles, it would take only about 2 per cent of Soviet missiles to destroy the US's main cities. President Bush is now going ahead with a revised version of 'star wars', but there's a great deal of scepticism that the money is going to be well spent. The fact remains that, for the first time in history, a powerful country is unable to defend its people from an attack.

Fourth, a new battlefield is developing: cyberspace. The US is training a squad of military and intelligence computer hackers who can defeat the US's enemies without a shot being fired. Instead, they will be able to plant computer viruses or 'logic bombs' in foreign networks to render them useless in wartime. Among the options are shutting down computerised energy air defence networks, shutting off power and telephone networks in major cities, feeding false data about troops and weapons deployment into enemy military information networks, and 'morphing' television propaganda into foreign networks. But the US, of course, as the world's main user of computers, is also highly vulnerable to these tactics being used against it.

Finally, it comes down to money. In 1990, when the Gulf War began, the US – despite all its wealth – had to put together a team of sponsors. Japan would not fight, but it agreed to help pay for those who were willing to do so, notably the US. Japan called the shots without having to fire them.

27

❓ What is the impact of the mass media on international politics?

The mass media – especially television – have a major impact on our lives: they're our window on the world. The amount of information we can know directly for ourselves is very limited. I know what I had for breakfast this morning because I was there at the time, but I don't know what happened in Washington or Moscow, say.

The power of the mass media has made English the international language of protest. In June 1989, the Chinese demonstrators in Tiananmen Square held placards explaining their views in English. English is hardly used in China outside the big cities, but that wasn't the point. The students weren't wanting to communicate with their fellow Chinese, but with people outside China who were watching on television – at that very instant.

The US-based Cable News Network (CNN) has led the way in the television news revolution. It broadcasts one signal instantly and continuously around the world; there is no delayed telecasting. In Australia, for example, Perth viewers get the ABC news two hours later than Sydney, to fit with Perth local time. But in CNN's world, there is only a twenty-four-hour clock. The technology is derived from communications satellites: a signal can be broadcast from a camera crew anywhere in the world to Atlanta, Georgia, in the US, edited, and then transmitted back around the world through the same network of communications satellites. Other stations, such as the BBC and Sky TV, now also provide instant and continuous news services.

This is all very different from the early 1960s, when signals were bounced off a single broadcasting satellite, Telstar. Not only that, it was necessary to wait for Telstar to move into the right position for the day so the signal could be bounced off it. The Vietnam War was the first war to be televised, but it wasn't 'live' television. The footage had to be flown to the US for broadcast.

The 1991 Gulf War was the first 'live' televised war. A US officer with the advancing forces, who had been given a free cellular telephone by the Saudi Government (another example of the information technology revolution), told me that he used to ring his wife in the US to find out what was going on. He felt she had a better overall view of the war from watching CNN, than someone like himself who was in the midst of it. Similarly, during that Gulf War the CIA complained that the then President Bush didn't read the CIA briefings. He said he preferred to watch CNN live because the written CIA briefings took a day to arrive.

Increased global transparency

The power of the mass media has also had a huge impact on global transparency. It's completely changed the Soviet tradition of secrecy, for example. Stalin could get away with his mass murders because they were done out of the media spotlight. Similarly, the USSR's first nuclear disaster (in the Urals in 1957) was hidden from foreign view for about two decades. By contrast, tragedies that occurred in Gorbachev's Soviet Union couldn't be so easily hidden from foreign view.

Gorbachev had been the Soviet leader for only about a year when the Chernobyl nuclear disaster took place on 26 April 1986. At first, Gorbachev employed the traditional Soviet technique of being slow to comment on the crisis, but it was known about overseas within hours because the radiation was detected and it was well televised – including by foreign satellite coverage, which was one of the first occasions such coverage was used. When Gorbachev eventually spoke about the disaster, on 14 May, he blamed the foreign media reporting an 'unrestrained anti-Soviet propaganda campaign'. Soviet citizens learned more about what was happening in the critical days after the Chernobyl explosion from the Voice of America radio broadcasting network and the BBC rather than from their own government. West Europeans were also critical of Gorbachev's inaction and he lost a great deal of the public sympathy he had acquired during his first year in office.

The disaster had a profound impact on Gorbachev. From that point on, natural disasters and human-made calamities would be reported promptly in the Soviet media. And after leaving office, Gorbachev established Green Cross, an international non-government organisation in Geneva that provides governments with the type of advice on how to handle environmental crises that he was unable to get in April 1986.

Incidentally, Gorbachev also had the flair of making television work for him. Unlike previous Soviet leaders, he was able to use US television to reach directly into US homes and so reduce the fears Americans had had about Soviet leaders since the Russian Revolution in 1917. US President Ronald Reagan was very good at staging an event – and upstaging the other leaders appearing with him – however, in December 1987 Gorbachev mounted his own charm offensive during his visit to the US. Much to the consternation of the Secret Service and the KGB, he conducted himself as if he were an American politician, and wherever he went crowds lined the streets to applaud him. He had a higher American approval rating than President Reagan himself.

East Timor is another example of the crucial importance of the mass media's ability to report on events as they happen. Until April 1974, East Timor was a neglected part of the Portuguese empire. Its fate was changed when the Armed Forces Movement took over power in Portugal and ended the dictatorship of Marcello Caetano. Portugal's new rulers couldn't get out of the colonies quickly enough, and East Timor came low on the list of the new Portuguese Government's priorities. Chaos at home and in the African colonies meant it had little time for sorting out East Timor's path to independence.

Indonesia invaded East Timor in December 1975. Indonesia is a fragile federation of 17,000 islands – about 3000 of which are inhabited – stretched out like a string of pearls across 5000 kilometres. The Indonesian Government's main problem is to hold the country together and a flourishing, independent East Timor might have inspired other parts of Indonesia that they too could survive as independent countries.

The invasion was a disaster, however. Indonesia expected a quick victory but it misjudged the skill of its own forces and underestimated the determination of the East Timorese to resist. In per capita terms, the war had one of the highest casualty rates of any war since 1945, but there was little mass media coverage of most of it.

East Timor started to become more visible in October 1989, with the visit of Pope John Paul II. The Pope did nothing to encourage the East Timorese to continue to resist the Indonesian invasion, but his mere presence in the capital, Dili, obliged the media to pay some attention to East Timor. The trip there to cover the Pope's visit sensitised them to East Timorese affairs.

On 12 November 1991, Indonesian forces fired into a crowd of people at the Santa Cruz cemetery in Dili. A memorial mass had been held there for Sebastiao Gomes, a youth shot dead by troops in an incident on 28 October, and the mass was followed by a pro-independence demonstration. Just what happened and how many mourners were killed remain unclear; it's also unclear as to who was behind the killings. The massacre was quite small compared with what had happened in the colony since 1975, but it was the first time any of the violence in East Timor had been captured on television.

The foreign journalists in Dili in November 1991 had been sent there to report on a long-awaited Portuguese Parliamentary Mission (which in fact was cancelled a few days prior to the massacre). One of the journalists, a New Zealander, was killed in the Santa Cruz massacre and an American journalist received a fractured skull (ironically, he was hit by a soldier using an American-made rifle). Journalists got film and radio coverage of the massacre back to the UK and US and then onto the international networks.

The Indonesian Government handled the media aftermath of the massacre badly. Previous East Timor massacres had come and gone, and there had been little international reaction; the government expected the same that time. It misunderstood the impact created by the film footage. The government conveyed an impression of being haphazard in finding out what had happened and in punishing those responsible. The mourners who took part in the protest at the cemetery received harsher prison sentences than did the soldiers who carried out the killings. As a result, in June 1992 the US Congress voted to reduce US aid to Indonesia.

Increased power for non-governmental organisations

Non-governmental organisations (NGOs) can now use the mass media to play to a global audience and exert overseas pressure on their government. For example, they may be able to deter foreign financial interests from investing in their country if the investors can 'see' how 'unstable' it is. Their struggle may become an international cause, such as the support given by other countries to the democratic cause of Chinese students.

Additionally, NGOs in other countries can see the links between international campaigns and their own agenda. These links create a global solidarity between NGOs and can provide common campaign themes, such as the successful fight in the 1980s to stop mining in Antarctica.

Starvation has been common throughout east Africa for at least the past few decades, but campaigns on this issue by development groups like World Vision, Oxfam and Community Aid Abroad were largely ignored by the mass media and the general public. In 1985, a BBC television crew, headed by Michael Buerk, was stranded in east Africa for a day because of aircraft problems. They went out for a walk and filmed the starvation and suddenly it became a media event. The Band Aid fundraising record and concert were organised as a direct result of that BBC coverage, in the hope that it would help the starving. In due course, however, the media became bored with the story. The issue was revived in 2005 with the Live 8 concert, but my fear is that Africa will again disappear from the front pages.

Making sense of the world

There's no doubt that the global media revolution has enabled us to see more of what's occurring around the world, but are we really learning more about those events? The news media aren't that well organised to deal with global issues and trends; they're often too compartmentalised. A news organisation has a number of 'desks' (or departments) to report and comment on events, such as those for politics, finance, entertainment and sport, and they each work separately. But, as this book has argued, global trends cut across national boundaries and therefore also often erode departmental lines. No one department can get a full picture of an event. Some trends fall through the gaps between the desks.

My Channel 7 *Sunrise* Global Notebook segments try to deal with three issues created by television's coverage of world affairs. It's vital that we have viewers who can cope with the challenges of global change, so it falls to the mass media to provide events in context.

No media: no event

Two months after the Tiananmen Square massacre in June 1989, Burmese protesters held a similar peaceful rally and up to 3000 were killed by troops. Why wasn't there the same sort of international outcry? Because of one significant difference: television cameras massed in Beijing for the historic visit of Russian President Mikhail Gorbachev were able to broadcast the Chinese massacre to the rest of the world and prompt international outrage. There were no cameras present to record the fate of the students, Buddhist monks, ordinary citizens and children killed in Burma. The event attracted comparatively little media attention.

An event takes place because the media are there to report it. If there are no media, there's no event.

28

? **How easy is it for governments to control the spread of information?**

The control of information is a standard theme in history. The rise of printing assisted the Protestant Reformation, as European Christians were able to get access to their own copies of the Bible in their own languages; many governments over the years have tried to censor information and issue propaganda; and generals have tried to distort the accounts of their battles. Some novels are also based on this theme, such as George Orwell's *1984*, where the bending of truth is overt, and Aldous Huxley's *Brave New World*, where the media make people comfortable consumers.

Perhaps the best example of how the UK has been changed by the global mass media is to examine an event that can never be repeated. When King George V died in early

1936, he was replaced by his playboy son, King Edward VIII, who was having an affair with an American woman, Mrs Simpson. She was in the process of getting divorced and so throughout 1936 the new King came under pressure from the British and most Commonwealth governments to give up any hope of eventually marrying her. It was the biggest political crisis of the year, but the British public knew very little about it until December 1936, when the King abdicated. He later married the American woman in France.

The reason the British public were kept in the dark was because the British newspaper owners all agreed to prevent any reference to the affair appearing in their newspapers, and the government controlled the only radio broadcaster, the BBC, and forbade it covering the crisis. The American media were awash with stories but little of this information reached the UK. It would be impossible now to hush up such a crisis for the best part of a year. At the very least, Britons would hear of it via foreign broadcasts into the UK.

It's a matter of speculation as to how television might have affected the conduct of trench warfare in World War I. If audiences at home had seen the appalling nature of that war, would there have been greater demand to end it more quickly?

During World War II, the Allied mass media were largely willing to accept censorship restrictions because there was agreement on the overall war aims. There was no such prolonged consensus during the Vietnam War. Vietnam was the first 'television war' because television crews were given considerable scope to report on it. The delay in getting film footage back to the US meant that it wasn't the first 'live' television war as such, but the graphic footage helped turn US public opinion against the war.

Ironically, it was this impact of mass media coverage of the Vietnam War that made the British Government determined to control the coverage of the 1982 Falklands War. The government limited the number of journalists accompanying the UK naval force and censored the material that was broadcast.

The US Government learnt from both its own experience in Vietnam and the UK Government's handling of the Falklands War when it came to planning the 1991 Gulf War coverage. Attacks and subsequent press conferences were timed to fit in with 'live' broadcasts back to the US for prime time television.

The first casualty in war has always been truth. The rise of a global mass media has simply meant that governments have faced a greater challenge in finding ways to censor or manipulate media coverage. They can do this most easily when their own country is involved in a conflict and so they can claim that media control is in the 'national interest'.

During the 1991 Gulf War, the impression gained from the media was that this was a highly sophisticated operation in which 'computer target' bombs were dropped on carefully chosen military targets with astonishing accuracy. The mass media scarcely questioned what the military authorities were saying. But when the war was over, Pentagon sources admitted that only 7 per cent of American explosives dropped during the Gulf War were 'computer target' bombs. Eventually it emerged that 70 per cent of the 88,500 tons of bombs dropped on Iraq and Kuwait missed their targets completely.

The Guardian newspaper in the UK reported over a year after the Gulf War ended that Allied ground forces during the war outnumbered the Iraqis by more than 3:1 at the start of the hostilities and that the Bush Administration had vastly overestimated the Iraqi military's fighting strength. This revelation came just after the Pentagon's admission that its so-called 'smart' bombs and Tomahawk cruise missiles weren't nearly as successful at hitting their intended targets as previously stated, and that the ground-launched Patriot missile, used against Iraqi Scud missiles, had also turned out to be less effective than advertised. Unfortunately, by the time these truths emerged, the attention of the media consumers had moved on.

Additionally, by the time these stories appeared, they were given limited time and space as television and the front pages of newspapers had become devoted to the latest issue of interest. 'Smart' bombs, for example, still retain their favourable image because the initial propaganda is what people remember, rather than the later, more balanced assessments of their limited effectiveness.

It's worth recalling what we now know about one of the most famous television scenes from the 1991 Gulf War. Shortly before the US Congress voted to go to war, a television report shook the nation: a girl, whose identity couldn't be revealed for fear of reprisals, sobbed as she reported the atrocities committed by Iraqi soldiers as they invaded Kuwait City. She described the sacking of the hospitals' paediatric departments, the destruction of incubators, the infants left to die on the floor. This was great television. Unfortunately, it wasn't true.

The interview was a fake; the interviewee was the daughter of the Kuwaiti ambassador in Washington, playing – with great talent – an imaginary role. One of America's leading communications agencies, financed by Kuwait, was behind this charade. Kuwait knew that it was an unpopular country in the Middle East and the US, so it hired a public relations company to draw the US into the war. Some of these events were later covered in the movie *Wag the Dog*.

29

❓ Is Taiwan a country?

In 2005, China reaffirmed its right to invade Taiwan if it declares independence. This is one of the most serious flashpoints in our region. The US is a supporter of Taiwan, and there's division within the Australian Government as to whether Australia's defence alliance with the US should include Australia lining up with the US against China.

China is undergoing the biggest economic expansion in world history. Not even the UK, which invented the Industrial Revolution 250 years ago, grew at the rate China is growing now. Why would China, with so much wealth to enjoy, want to squander that over a territorial dispute? Even odder is that Taiwan is one of the largest investors in China.

In 1895, a newly aggressive Japan took Taiwan from China following its war against the decaying Chinese imperial regime. Japan was preparing to build itself into a great power and this was one of its first conquests. Tokyo developed the colony of Taiwan and put this backwater on a firm economic footing.

Japan lost the colony after its defeat in World War II, and the US and UK agreed that Taiwan should be handed over to China. At that time, China was racked by civil war. The US backed Chiang Kai-shek's Kuomintang (KMT) Government against Mao Zedong's Communist insurgents, but in 1949 the Communists eventually won. Chiang and the remnants of his KMT regime fled to Taiwan. Even though they comprised only a minority of the population – about 14 per cent – they took over the island and ran it as a dictatorship. The KMT expected the Communists to fall from power quickly and saw their retreat to Taiwan as a temporary measure; they continued to call themselves the Republic of China. (The Communist Government calls its country the People's Republic of China.)

The US and its allies (including Australia) recognised the KMT on Taiwan as the Chinese Government for all of China, including the mainland and Taiwan. The KMT retained the Chinese seat at the United Nations and was one of the five permanent members of the UN Security Council. Every year, however, the Soviet Union and its allies tried to get mainland China recognised as the true ruler of China. The Communists and KMT agreed on one thing: there was only one China. The question was who ran it.

Australia (and many other non-Communist countries) got involved in all sorts of tangles over China. Politically, Australia followed the American line and supported Taiwan. But mainland China gradually increased in economic strength and became a market for Australian exports. Effectively, the Department of Foreign Affairs dealt with the KMT while the Department of Trade dealt with the Communists.

A turning point came in the early 1970s, when President Nixon was looking for a way out of the Vietnam War. He thought that improving relations with both the Soviet Union and China would result in their putting pressure on North Vietnam to take a softer line in the US–North Vietnam peace negotiations. Nixon had made his name partly as a tough anti-Communist in the 1950s and 1960s. He stunned the world by visiting China in 1972 and getting on well with Mao Zedong.

Taiwan suddenly felt very vulnerable. The USSR and its allies now had the numbers at the UN to push Taiwan out of China's seat and the Communists were allowed to enter the UN. Today, less than thirty countries still recognise the Republic of China.

But Taiwan itself was also changing. It became a 'newly industrialised country' with large foreign exchange reserves and was a pioneer in information technology. Gradually the emerging middle class wanted more of a say in how the country should be governed. In the early 1990s, the KMT Government permitted the rise of a democracy.

In 2000, the KMT lost power for the first time. Chen Shui-bian of the Democratic Progressive Party was elected President and re-elected in March 2004. President Chen – for the first time in presidential history – has questioned the 'one China' policy faithfully followed by both the Communists on the mainland and the KMT on Taiwan. Chen has suggested that Taiwan could go it alone; it could become an independent country with no claims on controlling mainland China.

He argues that China's 1.2 billion people are not going to overthrow the Communists and invite the KMT to resume power. Most people now living in China weren't even alive when the KMT ran the mainland. The KMT is history. Meanwhile, the 23 million people on Taiwan enjoy one of the world's highest standards of living. They could exist without having to think about regaining control of China.

Not all Taiwanese agree with President Chen's assessment. Many of them are willing to live with the ambiguity of neither complete independence nor complete control by China – particularly as they are doing well in the current situation. Taiwanese companies have over US$50 billion invested in China. About a million Taiwanese live in China running Taiwanese factories. They don't want politics interfering with their economic growth.

China itself retains the 'one China' policy. The country may be changing in many ways – not least economically and socially – but its views on Taiwan haven't changed since 1949.

President Bush is faced with a dilemma. His conservative political supporters want him to stand by Taiwan and oppose the Communist threats. But American business interests argue that Taiwan is a saturated market, while China is a vast untapped market for American goods. No doubt the Howard Government is also having its own private discussions about Australia's line on the question of whether to support China or Taiwan.

30

❓ Will Australia ever introduce an Australia Card?

Two or so decades ago, Canberra bureaucrats decided it would be a good idea to issue all Australians with some form of identity card. They first tried to sell the idea to the Fraser Government as a way of cracking down on 'dole bludgers'. When Labor came to power in 1983, the bureaucrats tried to argue that an identity card would be useful to crack down on wealthy tax cheats. In both cases, human rights activists were able to block the initiative.

Will the issue be revived in the light of the War on Terrorism? The British Government in late 2004 decided to start work on issuing such identity cards – a process that will take years to implement.

Australia has an ad hoc system of identity cards – driver's licences. But people like myself, who don't drive, have to resort to using passports. Given the way that Osama bin Laden has spooked Australia Post and the airline industry, I now need to take my passport to the post office to send a parcel overseas, or when I'm flying on a domestic passenger plane to, say, Tasmania or Melbourne.

I think it's only a matter of time before the Australia Card debate is revived in Australia.

31

❓ What is the relationship between Australia and the UK?

Australia is the second 'most English' country in the world, after England itself. Since 1788, the largest overseas-born group in Australia has been people from England. Many English people or people of English descent probably wouldn't regard themselves as an 'ethnic group': they are the norm; the rest are 'ethnics'. In 1996, New Zealanders replaced the English as the largest single immigrating group in Australia. Of course, many New Zealanders are themselves of English descent.

The links between Britain and Australia may be seen in two ways:

1. The debate over the republic.
2. Trade.

The debate over the republic

Queen Elizabeth II won her first election on 6 November 1999 when 54 per cent of Australians voted 'no' in a referendum on whether the country should become a republic. The monarchists were jubilant about the result, but it's important not to misread it. The referendum was based on the question of whether to change the Constitution so that a president would be elected by two-thirds of the national parliament. The people wouldn't have had any direct say in the selection of the president. Many people voted 'no' because of this, not because they wanted to retain links with the British monarchy.

The monarchy couldn't be defended on its merits. The Queen has little support in Australia and there's even less support for her children, their partners and ex-partners. According to opinion polls, only about 10 per cent of Australians want the Queen to stay on as the head of state. There's no spiteful antagonism; simply a sense of indifference towards her.

The republic debate was decided more by internal politics than by a resounding vote for maintaining the links with Britain; the vote was the most recent example of Australia's politics of anger. The monarchists didn't speak in favour of the Queen; they simply tapped into the loathing that many Australians feel for politicians, ruling elites and the urban rich. In the mid-1990s Pauline Hanson got a brief parliamentary career out of it. She's no longer in Parliament, but the anger she tapped into still exists and bubbles to the surface occasionally.

Australians have always been suspicious of authority figures. This attitude comes in part from the country's convict past and resonates in various ways across the community. The country's Indigenous peoples were dispossessed by the eighteenth-century British invasion and may not be keen on the Queen, but some voted against the referendum because it was seen as a proposal coming from the white elite. Australia's immense post-war immigration intake – which made it one of the top three most cosmopolitan countries in the world, along with Canada and Israel – included many people fleeing from authoritarian regimes. They may have little intrinsic love for the Queen but they don't like ruling elites either. A lot of people saw the issue as irrelevant to the country's main problems, such as the high level of foreign debt, unemployment, crime, alcohol and drug addiction, divorce and family breakdown. Ultimately, the voters rejected the referendum because they didn't like the people advocating it.

There's also the historical fact that in most referenda, Australians have acted conservatively. They generally vote 'no' in referenda; it's easier to stay with the status quo. Only about 20 per cent of referenda since 1901 have resulted in a 'yes' victory. Australians aren't conservative in all things. For example, they're innovative and have a great love for all forms of new technology. It's just in politics that they're suspicious: they don't want rapid change foisted upon them by politicians. The 6 November 'no' vote enabled them to keep their options open. They can return to the republic question in the future.

The republican groups themselves were divided on the issue: some supported the vote and others did not. Among the opponents were republicans who claimed it would be better to have a directly elected president, rather than one decided on by the politicians. These people voted 'no' in the hope of getting a popularly elected president later on in a more ambitious campaign. This lack of agreement among republican groups added to the worry of some voters, who voted 'no' because the issue seemed so complicated. Success in a referendum requires political unanimity.

Australia is now in a republic deadlock. There are four reasons for this:

1. The Queen has little support in Australia. There is a residual, if very low-key, republican feeling.
2. Some of the 1901 Constitution no longer makes much sense. For example, it contains no reference to a 'prime minister' or 'cabinet' or 'local government' and is written very much in terms of the Governor-General running the country. Therefore, the real issue isn't the head of state but the need to modernise the entire Constitution. For example, Australia is one of the most over-governed countries in the western world. There is one Australian politician for every 930 electors, whereas the UK has one politician for every 22,000 electors (though this may change now the UK is acquiring a taste for devolved government). Tasmania is said to have more politicians per capita than anywhere else in the world. If the Australian loathing of politicians were taken to its logical conclusion, a result would be a reduction in the total number of politicians.
3. The monarchists didn't win the 6 November referendum; the republicans lost it. Their squabbling created the opportunity for the monarchists to shift the attention off the Queen and on to the disunity within the republicans. A basic issue of disagreement was the method of electing the president: some republicans voted 'no' because they wanted a popularly elected president, not one selected by politicians. Opinion polls showed that if Australia were to become a republic, then 70 per cent of the people want to elect the president, rather than leave it to politicians. But a popularly elected head of state would raise many complicating issues. For example, would that

person then have more power than the Governor-General – so moving towards a US model? Given that the best-organised bodies for national elections are political parties, then fairly quickly the candidates for such office would be party nominees and so the presidency would be held by a politician. That prospect would scare off many potential supporters for Constitutional change because they loathe politicians.

4. The low level of political literacy in Australia. More than 80 per cent of Australians have virtually no understanding of the current system of government. Successive governments have failed to have any form of civics taught in Australian schools, and politics is seen as having little relevance to the ordinary person. Australia is one of the few developed countries where it is compulsory to vote; failure to do so is a crime. Forty-one people went to prison in 1996 for failing to vote. Voters often see politicians as people who go into politics to line their own pockets. Indeed, it seems that at any one time there is at least one politician at state or federal level who is under investigation, on trial or in prison. It would be interesting to examine the rates of criminality among politicians compared with the population at large.

The bottom line seems to be that Australia is stuck with its link with the British monarchy, not because it likes it but because it's difficult to see what the alternative would be.

Trade

The British acquired most of their sprawling empire in an indirect way: the flag followed trade. Seventeenth- and eighteenth-century traders went in search of foreign markets and did deals with local rulers; they weren't trying to convert the world into becoming Britons. In the nineteenth century, British influence was solidified by direct British rule. The British 'tribe' dwelling around the globe provided what was then the world's best financial network.

Australia, ironically, was the main exception to this trade-driven imperialism: it was claimed and settled via government projects – such as establishing Sydney as a place to stick convicts. Then its economic potential was discovered and Australia began to supply raw materials and food for the British market. For example, in the 1870s Australia became the world's biggest supplier of wool. For years, wool was the country's principal source of wealth, thereby giving rise to the statement that 'Australia rides on the sheep's back'. Australia remains the world's largest exporter of wool. In the 1890s, 80 per cent of world trade was in primary products – the world wanted what Australia could easily produce. At the beginning of the twentieth century, Australia probably had the world's highest standard of living. It therefore did very well out of its traditional British trading link.

But in 1973 Britain entered what is now the European Union and Australia focused far more on its Asian trading partners, and so began a gradual growing apart. This wasn't done with any anger or bitterness; it's simply that the two countries have different priorities and economic allies.

Australia now has different links for different purposes; its eggs are no longer just in the British basket. It remains linked politically to the British monarchy; its trade is with a variety of countries in Asia; and its main defence ally is the United States.

32

❓ What is 'free trade'?

This is one of the most controversial areas of economic policy. Opinion has remained divided over it for centuries. In general, I'm a supporter of free trade, but I recognise that there are some problems with it.

The theory of free trade is that each country should specialise in what it does best, and that goods and services can be traded across national boundaries so all consumers have access to the world's supplies. World trade is growing faster than national economies. In other words, countries are doing more trade with each other as the years go by, and are doing so at a faster rate than their own national economic growth.

Countries are richer as a result of international free trade. This is because a country can do less of the things that don't make sense for its economy and more of the things that do. A small country like Australia, for example, can't be as clever in as many industries or have the economies of scale of bigger countries with bigger home markets, such as the US or the European Union.

The alternative policy to free trade is 'protection', where a country protects its own producers. The options for protection include:

- Tariffs – a tax imposed on imported goods and commodities to make them more expensive and so encourage citizens to buy local goods or commodities instead.
- Subsidies – a government payment made to reduce the cost of a local good or commodity to make it cheaper than foreign versions and provide an incentive for citizens to buy local items.
- Import licensing – where the importation of goods or commodities is restricted to a specified number of importers.
- Customs duty – a government can protect its own industries by claiming that the operation of its customs and quarantine departments necessitates the imposition of a customs duty on imported items to recoup the cost of the service. However, customs duties are often seen, especially by overseas competition, as a disguised form of tariffs.

Free trade is 'free' in that it's not subject to import tariffs or quotas. The goods and services aren't 'free' in the normal sense of the word – there's still a price to be paid. Indeed, if you're a domestic producer, you could claim that the price is extremely high – your job.

Free trade is divisive simply because there are no clear-cut answers. One problem with international free trade agreements – each of which increases the level of world trade – is that the benefits are dispersed among the general population while the disadvantages are concentrated on a particular minority. For example, a reduction in farm protection would enable the general population of a country to buy their produce – from home or overseas – more cheaply, but this would be at the disadvantage of their own farmers. Farming non-governmental organisations are good at lobbying (especially in Western Europe and the US) to protect their industry.

There is also the problem of balancing advantages and disadvantages. For example, Australia gradually reduced tariffs on textiles. This was to the advantage of Australian consumers who could buy clothes more cheaply, but to the disadvantage of the already heavily hit Australian textile industry and its workers, who lost jobs.

International free trade

Republican Herbert Hoover was elected as US President in 1928. He ran on a protectionist ticket, promising US farmers that he would shut out cheap food imports at a time when world agriculture was in recession. Hoover signed the Smoot–Hawley Tariff Act, raising US import duties on farm products to record levels. This resulted in a collapse in world trade and commodity prices, leading to a two-thirds contraction in world trade, and so contributed to the Great Depression of the 1930s. As a large exporting country, the US effectively undermined its own industrial exports with agricultural protection. The Democrats, on the other hand, advocated free trade and Roosevelt (who became President four years later) blamed the world recession partly on Hoover and the Smoot–Hawley tariffs.

Germany was hit particularly hard by the Depression. Before the Depression Hitler was just one of several extremist politicians with a small following and few people took him seriously. But the economic crisis gave him a sudden window of opportunity to rise to power in January 1933. The Depression, therefore, contributed to World War II.

The United Nations, which was created in 1945 towards the end of the war, saw economic reform as a major objective and was committed to the encouragement of free trade. The diplomats proposed the creation of an International Trade Organization (ITO) to encourage trade. The US Congress opposed the plan because it thought the ITO would hinder the US's own global economic expansion, and so the idea lapsed.

As a temporary measure, the General Agreement on Tariffs and Trade (GATT) was negotiated in 1947. By this time the Cold War was under way and all the Soviet bloc countries were boycotting the UN's economic activities. (Only with the end of the Cold War have Russia and the East European countries become involved in these activities.) GATT therefore consisted of the rich western developed countries and pro-western Third World countries. GATT members were responsible for about 90 per cent of world trade.

Membership of GATT was not automatic; countries had to negotiate to join. If a country joined, then it promised that all other GATT member-countries would be treated equally in world-trade matters or that none should be discriminated against – the so-called 'most-favoured-nation' principle. When it was recognised that the international rules governing trade were in need of revision, the new rules had to provide for the mutual benefit of all concerned parties; that is, revisions were to be negotiated on the basis of reciprocity. GATT member-countries therefore agreed to the principles of non-discrimination and reciprocity: there should be no special favourites or victims in the trading policies of member-countries. If two GATT countries negotiated a special trading arrangement, then that had to be offered to all the other GATT member-countries.

GATT progressed by a series of negotiations, which eventually resulted in tariffs being reduced. These negotiations were so lengthy that cynics said 'GATT' stood for 'General Agreement to Talk and Talk'. But the delays were a reflection of the power of domestic NGOs, which wanted to stall free trade in order to protect their own industries.

Nowadays, international free trade is the mood of the moment. GATT has been replaced by an even more ambitious organisation: the World Trade Organization (WTO). Its work includes items not previously addressed, such as banking and computer software.

33

❓ Does Australia win or lose from free trade?

Australia has had its own rocky history of free trade – even between the colonies that created the Commonwealth of Australia. Trade barriers were very important for the post-1788 development of Australia because they protected the creation of Australian manufacturing industries. The protection–free trade debate was part of the turmoil leading up to – and almost derailing – Federation in 1901. The colony of Victoria, which had the manufacturing base, opted for protection, while NSW, which was more based on the export of commodities, went for free trade. The Victorian model prevailed in the new Commonwealth for the first seven decades and so the new country of the Commonwealth of Australia was a protectionist country.

The change began tentatively in the early 1970s, with

the election of the Labor Government under Gough Whitlam (1972–75). It was a difficult issue because the Labor Party and the labour movement were as divided on the issue of protection as was the then Liberal Party.

In the 1980s, the Hawke Labor Government (first elected in 1983) decided it had no choice but to subject the Australian economy to greatly increased global influences. The drastic reform process could have been carried out in a less dramatic way if it had commenced decades earlier. But government and mass media attention had been focused elsewhere: farming and mining seemed to be going well, and foreign policy was dominated by military considerations (notably the Cold War). There had been no incentive to address the larger questions of Australia's overall sense of economic strategy. By 1983, when the incoming Hawke Labor Government began to examine the strategy, the process of globalisation and free trade was well under way and so the government was forced into the changes.

The Hawke Government economic reforms of the 1980s were the largest reforms since 1901. They included:

- complete deregulation of the financial sector, including floating the currency and the introduction of foreign banks
- reform of the tax system
- a tariff reduction program
- promotion of competition and planning of national infrastructure, especially in the areas of power, roads, rail, waterfront, aviation, telecommunications and industrial relations
- industry policy initiatives to promote global competitiveness in agriculture, other primary industries, manufacturing and services

- the commercialisation of government services
- the privatisation of some assets (such as the Commonwealth Bank)
- support for enhanced education and training.

The government thought that global competition would force Australian companies to do better or force them out of business. Indeed, some companies flourished and some failed. Some new industries opened up or expanded further, such as tourism, while others, such as parts of the clothing manufacturing industry, virtually disappeared.

The current Howard Government is a continuation of the philosophy of the Hawke/Keating Labor Governments. In terms of economic history, it's likely to be remembered mainly for the introduction of the GST (which Treasurer Paul Keating first attempted in the Hawke Labor Government). But other than that, its economic policy will simply be seen as a footnote to those of the preceding Labor Governments.

The prevailing view now is that protection did harm to Australia, especially in the post-1945 period, and had to be ended. All the major Australian political parties are supporters of international free trade, though they still have their internal debates.

Just trade, green trade

One impact of the international trading order is the potential conflict between trading policy and human rights policy. Workers' rights are jeopardised in the interests of making money. In many developing countries, people work in very unsatisfactory conditions. In China, for example, camps for political prisoners are run as factories to produce goods to sell to developed countries.

One response is to restrict the importation of products from such countries until they lift their human rights standards. But such a response may become illegal under the new WTO world-trade treaty because such measures could be seen as 'non-tariff barriers to trade'. For example, China may try to claim that any human rights restrictions are simply a way of keeping out goods that would undercut the prices in developed countries.

Environmental groups in the US have already seen the impact of non-tariff barriers to trade. Tuna fishing has become big business since a new system of nets (purse seine) was invented in the 1950s. Canned tuna is now a staple in the US diet. The US 1972 Marine Mammal Protection Act bans the sale of tuna caught by domestic or foreign fishers who also catch dolphins in their purse-seine nets. The US used this legislation to ban Mexican cans of tuna, but Mexico complained to then GATT, arguing that the law was a non-tariff barrier to trade. GATT accepted the Mexican claim. Mexico decided not to press its victory because it wanted the North American Free Trade Agreement (NAFTA) to go ahead and so could not afford to alienate the US. But Mexico's victory was not overlooked by US environmentalists, who see the victory as a poor omen.

There is a very real risk that future negotiations on new world-trade agreements will result in a levelling down – rather than a levelling up – of human rights and environmental standards. Therefore, the gains made in human rights and environmental legislation will be reduced.

34

? Why is Indonesia the 'crippled giant' of South East Asia?

Indonesia is a country of immense natural resources, such as oil and natural gas. The ground is fertile and so no one should starve there. 'Poke a stick in the ground and something will grow,' say the Javanese on the country's main island. Indonesia's post-independence history has been characterised by turbulence, repression and corruption. Following its recent relatively peaceful revolution, it is now the third-largest democracy in the world (after India and the United States), but its potential strength has not been achieved. It is now making some economic progress, but at considerable political and social cost, both of which threaten the country's stability.

Indonesia consists of 17,000 islands located on one of the main sea routes running through Asia and into the

Pacific. Its east–west axis is the equivalent of the distance between London and New York and covers three time zones. The Indonesian islands have had a variety of visitors over thousands of years, many of whom have left their distinctive characteristics. Indonesia's national motto is 'bhinneka tunggal ika' (unity in diversity). Its history and present policies all have a bearing on or are influenced by the need to maintain national unity.

The history of Indonesia

The early Asian traders not only sought commerce; they also brought Hindu priests who were seeking converts. From the fourteenth century onwards, the Hindu and Buddhist cultures, especially on Sumatra and Java, were overcome by the spread of Islam as more traders came looking for spices and carrying a new faith. With about 10 per cent of the world's Muslims, Indonesia is the world's most populous Islamic country, though it also contains some adherents of the earlier faiths.

The next religious overlay was Christianity, brought by the Portuguese. They had difficulty breaking the monopoly held by the traders and priests from China, India and Islamic countries. Instead of trying to supplant existing religious and commercial arrangements, the Portuguese encouraged trade and won converts in the other parts of the archipelago.

It's worth noting that each invader up to this time didn't try to create the country of 'Indonesia' as such, but was content to occupy corners of it. While Indonesia is an old country in terms of its original inhabitants and its impact on the international trading system, it's not old at all in terms of being a unified political whole.

The Dutch had more success in gaining political and economic control over what is now Indonesia. Much of the Netherlands' nineteenth-century prosperity was derived from the Dutch East Indies. (The old international reputation of the Spice Islands' wealth can be seen in Christopher Columbus' 1492 voyage: he arrived in the Americas, but was actually seeking a quicker route to the Spice Islands.) When the British began to increase their influence in the region – from India (present-day Pakistan, India, Bangladesh and Burma) to the north-west, Singapore and Malaysia to the north, and Australia and New Zealand to the south-east – the Dutch feared Britain would also seek to control part of their Spice Islands. This gave them an incentive to acquire greater political control over the region, rather than just controlling trading relations.

Along with their suspicions of British ambition, the Dutch had the greater problem of colonial revolts. Java was most rebellious, especially in the periods 1825–30 and 1894–99. The conflict continued into the twentieth century, with a major – if abortive revolt – in 1926. Some negotiations on a form of limited self-government took place prior to World War II, but didn't come to fruition.

The weakness of support for the Dutch colonisers was shown by the relative ease with which the Japanese were able to establish control over the colonies from December 1941. Many inhabitants saw the Japanese as liberators, which, ironically, they turned out to be because World War II marked the end of Dutch control.

Independence was declared on 17 August 1945 by Indonesian nationalists. The Dutch didn't recognise the independence and made a brutal yet futile effort to regain control. On 27 December 1949, the Dutch surrendered sovereignty to the Republic of Indonesia – except for West

Papua, which was left temporarily under Dutch control until its future could be decided.

Achmed Sukarno, founder of the Indonesian Nationalist Party in 1927 and the leading figure in the fight for independence, was the first President of Indonesia (until 1965). He was a charismatic and inspiring figure and ruled with his own blend of Marxism, nationalism, Islam and traditional Javanese concepts. He was one of the founders of the Third World bloc in international politics.

Sukarno was involved in the original debate on what should constitute 'Indonesia'. Some of the nationalists argued that the new country should consist solely of Java and immediate islands. Others – including Sukarno – said that the entire Dutch empire should be incorporated into the new country. That decision has haunted Indonesian politics ever since. Can any single government in Jakarta control such a vast and diverse group of islands and people?

Indonesia's economic future

Indonesia, with 210 million people, is the world's fourth most populous country and the largest country in South East Asia. It's a reasonable place to invest, and is recovering from the 1997 Asian economic crisis. Profit-making isn't without its difficulties – companies must deal with bloated bureaucracies, corruption and a complex society where business depends heavily on personal relations – but the rewards make all this worthwhile.

Indonesia is deliberately enticing foreign investment. Labour conditions are harsh and pay rates are low. Trade unions are weak, government officials are cooperative (provided the bribe is large enough), the country has immense natural resources and there are few environmental restrictions. Consequently, Indonesia is now becoming a centre for export manufacturing. Companies from Japan, South Korea, Taiwan and the US have established factories there to produce such items as clothes, sports shoes and radios for the world.

Meanwhile, Indonesia is becoming the 'real thing' according to the former president of Coca-Cola, Donald Keough: 'When I think of Indonesia, a country on the equator, with [then] 200 million people, a median age of eighteen, and a Muslim ban on alcohol, I feel like I know what heaven looks like.'

Economic change globally tends to bring about demands for political and social change. The Indonesian experience may be seen in two ways:

1. The risk to social harmony because of the growing gap between rich and poor.
2. The push from more affluent members of society to have a say in how the country is run.

Indonesia has to create 2.1 million jobs a year for new entrants to the labour market. Indonesians are increasingly living in an urban environment saturated by advertisements for consumer goods that they know they stand little chance of obtaining. Meanwhile, more than 48 per cent of urban dwellers in Jakarta still have no access to potable water, primary health care and other social services. The urban poor constitute one of the most important factors in determining Indonesia's future.

A rallying point for dissent in many Third World countries is the fringe Islamic parties. They can address their male adherents regularly each Friday at the mosques, and promise a better way of life if the adherents will support them. In earlier decades, the main opponents of a government such as Indonesia's would have been the Communists; now they are Muslims. The Indonesian Government can't ban Muslims from congregating, but it does try to monitor their behaviour.

There is a seething resentment in Indonesia towards the people who are getting rich quickly – particularly the Chinese – and there have been acts of violence in various places across the country in recent years.

The conflict in Aceh

The Aceh conflict is an example of some of the difficulties the central Indonesian Government in Jakarta has in trying to hold the country together.

Until early 2005, when it was so badly hit by the tsunami, Aceh had been off limits to foreign human rights organisations. Jakarta is trying to stop the war of independence there and didn't want foreign observers seeing what was happening. For example, in late 2004 the Australian section of the International Commission of Jurists – of which I am the New South Wales Chairperson – received a visiting team of female Acehnese lawyers to brief us on the human rights situation. When they returned to Indonesia, they were arrested and imprisoned in an underground gaol. They were all drowned when the tsunami washed through their city.

The war in Aceh is probably the longest-running in this region. It began in 1873 and has continued on and off ever since. Originally, the Acehnese fought the Dutch; now they're fighting the national Indonesian Government in Jakarta. There's no obvious end to the conflict.

Aceh has long been geographically important. It lies on the western tip of the giant island of Sumatra, and is also at the mouth of the Malacca Straits – between Indonesia and Malaysia – which is one of the world's most important waterways. Aceh was the gateway to the 17,000 other islands in what is now called Indonesia and was therefore the first part of that country to have contact with the outside world.

Arab traders took Islam to the area in about the twelfth century, possibly even earlier, and people of Arab descent continue to live along Aceh's coast. Other people, also mainly on the coast, have Indian, Chinese or European origins. They all reflect the territory's history as an important trading area.

Aceh was a popular trading location: it was in the right place at the right time. Traders going to present-day Indonesia or China or elsewhere in eastern Asia all passed by. In 1292, European explorer Marco Polo visited Aceh on his epic journey to China. He reported on the busy trading activities of its ports. Other Europeans began arriving in the area in the sixteenth century, beginning with the Portuguese in 1509.

Aceh's dominance in trade and politics peaked around 1610–40, before the Europeans started to try to control the region. Aceh had its own diplomats in overseas capitals and was recognised by other countries as an independent country. It had its own navy and army.

Later, the British and Dutch started competing for influence in the region. The British claimed Aceh as a territory even though they had little real control over it. Eventually, in 1824, the British agreed with the Dutch to stop trying to get control of present-day Indonesia, while the Dutch agreed to stop trying to get control over India and Singapore. However, the Dutch then found that actually gaining control over Aceh was a lot more difficult than they had expected. The Acehnese were proudly independent and resisted any foreign control.

The Dutch formally declared war on Aceh on 26 March 1873. The Aceh War, which ran until 1942, was the longest and bloodiest colonial war the Dutch ever fought. The Dutch lost about 10,000 people, while as many as 100,000 Acehnese were killed. The war only ended because the Japanese entered World War II and invaded the Dutch East Indies.

Indonesian nationalists decided to use World War II as an opportunity to work for national independence and they invented 'Indonesia'. There was a major debate as to where the boundaries of their new country should be drawn. Some just wanted the island of Java and the immediate vicinity as the new Indonesia, so the country would comprise people of a similar culture and religion, making it easier to govern. Others wanted to claim all of the Dutch East Indies, which would mean more people and more territory – even though it would be difficult to create a unified sense of national identity. The second point of view was eventually accepted by the nationalists. Today, Indonesia has about 360 tribal groups and 250 languages.

Following Japan's defeat and Indonesia's independence, the new government sent troops into Aceh to ensure that the people recognised Jakarta's authority. The Aceh War broke out again, this time against a new enemy.

In 1959, Jakarta backed down a bit by granting Aceh 'special territory' status: it would remain within Indonesia but would have a lot more say in running its own affairs. This reduced some of the fighting, but many Acehnese still wanted to return to their own national independence.

Since 1959, the fighting has often flared up and died down. Before the tsunami struck, Aceh was largely inaccessible for foreign journalists and human rights monitors and so it was difficult to assess the severity of the fighting. However, it was assumed that this was the area of some of the worst violence in Indonesia, with the Indonesian military still unable to get control of all the territory.

The organisation fighting the military is known as the Free Aceh Movement (GAM). Many Acehnese support GAM for four reasons:

1. They want to maintain their tradition of independence. They don't want to be ruled by people outside their territory.
2. Acehnese Muslims are stricter than Muslims in most of the rest of Indonesia and want to maintain that religious zeal. Indonesia is an important Islamic country but it's not a formal Islamic state. Its founders in 1945 wanted a more secular country and took Turkey as a model, rather than Saudi Arabia or Iran. Conservative Islamic leaders in Indonesia don't like Aceh's Islamic zeal and have condemned GAM for disrupting national unity. The Acehnese Muslims aren't fundamentalists, however – they have no history of association with terrorist groups such as al-Qai'da and Jema'ah Islamiyah (JI). Indeed JI – the group responsible for the 2002 Bali bombing – wouldn't be popular with GAM because it wants to create a new Islamic state incorporating parts of Indonesia, southern Malaysia and the southern Philippines. GAM wants national independence; it doesn't want to be incorporated into any other larger entity.
3. Aceh is angry because it sees so little of its own wealth. The territory has only about 4 million people (out of a total population of over 210 million) but is one of the wealthiest parts of Indonesia because of oil, natural gas

and other resources. Aceh is responsible for about 15 per cent of Indonesia's total exports. On a per capita basis, the Acehnese are potentially very rich, but little of that wealth stays in the territory. GAM believes Aceh would be able to finance itself very well as an independent country.

4. About two-thirds of Indonesia's population is concentrated on its fifth largest island, Java. The Indonesian Government has tried to solve its country's population problems by implementing a 'transmigration' policy: moving people away from the most crowded locations to live elsewhere, including Aceh. The Acehnese complain that, as an incentive to move, the Indonesians get preferential treatment in employment. The Acehnese also fear that the mass arrival of the Javanese means the arrival of Javanese culture and the erosion of their own culture.

There is no obvious way to end the Aceh War. The Acehnese aren't going to surrender and accept Jakarta's control; and Jakarta can't afford to allow Aceh to regain its independence. The territory is too economically important for Jakarta to lose its revenue. Also, independence in Aceh would inspire other parts of the country (such as West Papua) to continue their own struggle for independence.

35

❓ Are environmental problems a threat to world peace?

They can be. In some countries in Africa, for example, the expanding desert or soil erosion will do more to undermine national security than an invading army could ever do.

'National security' shouldn't be defined only in terms of the percentages of gross national product spent on defence, and armed forces alone shouldn't be viewed as the sole guarantors of national security because the real threats to national security go beyond military ones. A new concept of 'environmental security' has emerged from the relationship between the environment and armed conflict. This relationship has existed for centuries, but it's only in the last few years that the problem has become acute enough to force a fresh consideration of the two matters.

There are four main links between the environment, national security and world peace:

1. The environment as a cause of conflict.
2. Environmental destruction as a cause of armed conflict.
3. The environment as a victim of conflict.
4. The environment as a beneficiary of peace.

The environment as a cause of conflict

The environment itself has long been a cause of conflict. Thousands of years ago, tribes invaded the territory of other tribes to settle on the land and exploit it. The quest for fresh territory has always been a motive of imperialism.

The era of European imperialism has ended but its consequences remain: there are almost forty major boundary disputes in existence around the world as a direct result of European colonisation. For example, colonists often used rivers as boundaries between national claims, while the original inhabitants regarded the rivers as highways running through their settlements – they were like Australian families living either side of a main road. Suddenly, the tribes were divided up into different European nationalities. Such boundaries were often imprecise and are inadequate for today's nation-state boundaries.

In a resource-hungry world, environmental disputes are likely to increase. Take the problem of water in the Middle East: few issues are more central to life than the provision of adequate supplies of water, and few issues have been more neglected in discussions of the Middle East situation than the question of water. The longest-running active conflict in the late twentieth century was ostensibly over the control of a river, although many doubt that was the true cause of the Iran–Iraq war in the 1980s.

Jordan and Israel are in dispute over the Jordan River system, for both technical and political reasons. The Jordan

River system – which is shared by four riparian states: Israel, Jordan, Syria and Lebanon – has a very complex hydrological structure in terms of its water balance, its outflows and run-offs, its sources and springs and so on. Those four riparian states are also hostile towards one another and have been for about two generations. The political situation is complicated even further by the overarching Israeli–Palestinian problem. Taken together, these factors have so far made it difficult to reach an agreement on the cooperative utilisation of the Jordan system.

Since 1948 there have been no less than fourteen schemes put forward by the US, Jordan, Israel, the United Nations, the World Zionist Organization and the Arab League for sharing and developing the waters of the River Jordan. None of these schemes, regardless of how workable or how sensible, has ever been adopted.

With about 200 river basins worldwide shared by two or more countries, the Middle East water problems are an example of what's likely to become an even greater cause of conflict in the future.

Environmental destruction as a cause of armed conflict

Environmental destruction itself can contribute to an armed conflict. The distinction between this link and the first isn't necessarily clear-cut: both involve people moving from one territory into another. The difference is more one of motivation: instead of a small number of colonialists setting out for a new life elsewhere, and leaving many of their citizens back home, a whole group has to move because its present location is too damaged to sustain life. They don't necessarily want to move; they're forced to because of the decline of their local environment.

One example of this is Ethiopia. By the early 1970s, the country's traditional highland farming area was losing soil. This led to food shortages in the cities and the ensuing disorder helped precipitate the overthrow of Emperor Haile Selassie in 1974. Environmental problems were not the whole story; several other factors contributed, notably economic incompetence, institutional rigidity, social inequity and the political repression of Emperor Selassie's regime. But food prices were the final factor that triggered the crisis, which in turn reflected long-gathering but little-recognised factors of environmental decline.

Subsequently, the new regime under Mengistu Haile Mariam didn't move fast enough to restore agriculture. As a result, throngs of impoverished peasants began streaming into the country's lowlands – including the Ogaden zone straddling the border with Somalia, an area of long-standing dispute between the two countries. Hostilities broke out in 1977. Again, the environmental factor was far from being the sole contributor to Mengistu's woes; rather, it worked to compound the adverse repercussions of political and military struggles within his regime, as well as the regime's preoccupation with Tigré and Eritrea provinces and a general political instability. Reacting to all of these elements combined, the Somalis invaded Ethiopia to stop the peasant migration into its territory and violence continues to this day in that part of east Africa. Mengistu fled to Zimbabwe in May 1991.

A second example comes from the speculation over climate change because of the 'greenhouse effect'. Assuming that the planet does become warmer, the sea will expand (because heat makes all substances expand) and it's possible that even the Arctic and Antarctic ice may melt. Rising sea levels will necessitate the migration of low-level shore-based communities to higher ground. These 'environmental refugees' will need to move into other people's territory.

Another distinction between this link and the first is the perception of the problem. A colonial invasion was quickly obvious to the original inhabitants: the colonisers were there to stay and expected cooperation from the original inhabitants. Environmental refugees (like all refugees) see their migration as only temporary and not as an act of colonisation. In due course, they hope to return to their homeland. The original inhabitants may have some sympathy for these refugees initially, but this is likely to turn to hostility once it becomes clear they can't return to their own territory. If current concern about environmental refugees is correct, then this problem is likely to increase.

The environment as a victim of conflict

All armed conflicts have been fought between humans, with humans and the local environment as victims of the conflict. There's nothing new here except that the application of modern technology to warfare has made the potential or actual destruction far greater than in previous centuries.

The environment becomes a victim in three ways:

1. In the preparation for armed conflict, such as the erection of fortifications and nuclear-weapon testing. Ironically, as some European monuments attest, some fortifications have lasted longer than the rulers who built them – Europe's castles and France's Maginot line, for example. Nuclear testing's contribution – especially prior to the 1963 Partial Test Ban Treaty – has been to

scatter radioactive debris over an area well beyond the testing ground itself, especially via the atmosphere.
2. Virtually every armed conflict in history has resulted in environmental damage, such as the destruction of food stocks and the poisoning of water supplies. 'Scorched earth' policies – the deliberate removal or destruction of everything that might be useful to an invading army – are nothing new: classical Greek writers reported on them over 2000 years ago. The contemporary threat is the enhanced scope for destroying a much greater section of the environment, especially via nuclear weapons.
3. The problem of cleaning up after a conflict. Battlefields themselves have remarkable regenerative capabilities – as is evident from France to the Urals. However, unexploded ordnance remains a danger well after any conflict. For example, the USS *Montgomery*, an ammunition ship that ran ashore in 1944, still lies in the mouth of the River Thames in England. The British authorities decided to leave the ammunition on board where it's gradually rotting away – although no one is willing to go on board to check. In the early 1990s, after the reunification of the two Germanys, Berlin was rebuilt in readiness to become the national capital once again. Some builders were killed when they accidentally triggered unexploded World War II bombs on old sites.

The Afghanistan conflict has left many 'booby traps' and land mines scattered around the countryside. The International Red Cross has estimated that, at the current rate of clearing land mines, the country won't be clear for another two centuries. This means that it's possible for someone laying a land mine to accidentally kill their grandchildren or even great-grandchildren in the future.

Land mines are 'silent sentries': always on duty and ready to explode. Modern technology has made the problem of finding and clearing land mines even more difficult. Some anti-personnel land mines are made from plastic and can't be tracked down by metal detectors. Also, metal detectors are unable to distinguish a bomb or mine that failed to explode from the metal shreds of one that did.

While discussing this problem of unexploded ordnance in South Vietnam in 1974, I was informed about the problem caused by the chemical defoliants that had been dropped to kill vegetation and so expose combatants using it for cover. The defoliants tended to kill the weaker vegetation, which allowed the stronger vegetation to grow more easily since it had less competition for nutrients. But the growth of the stronger vegetation made the later detection of unexploded ordnance even more difficult. One way of disposing of the unexploded ordnance was to set the vegetation ablaze, as intense heat sometimes triggered the devices. In order to save the environment it was necessary first to destroy it.

Now that some progress is being made in nuclear and chemical disarmament, we also have the problem of disposing of weapons of mass destruction outlawed by the new agreements. For example, toxic chemical agents can't be disposed of simply by dumping them at sea; they need to be incinerated at high temperatures. The disposal process itself is controversial – where will the incinerators be located? – and there's the question of how to transport the agents to the incineration sites.

The environment as a beneficiary of peace

Finally, there's the fact that the environment could benefit from an absence of armed conflict. A reduction in military expenditure, for example, could be spent in soil conservation, planting trees, and protecting coastal nations from flood.

Bangladesh is often affected by coastal flooding. When trees high up in the Himalayas are cut down, the loss of tree roots means the soil can no longer be held in place; when the snow melts it carries the loose soil down into Bangladesh delta, where it silts up and causes flooding in another country. The problem of coastal flooding has long been identified, but the high cost of the engineering complexities needed to fix it has blocked action. The World Bank has recommended a US$25 billion program to prevent annual floods each year in the lowlands of India and Bangladesh, which would also need to involve Nepal and possibly China in what would be one of the world's largest engineering projects. The US Army Corps of Engineers is one of the world's largest and oldest engineering companies. If peace were to break out, there would be less need for military engineering activities and so the Army Corps of Engineers could become involved in the Bangladesh flood plan.

We can make a similar point about irrigation systems in Africa: the frequent droughts in Africa aren't so much due to a shortage of water as to the lack of adequate irrigation systems. If military engineers were no longer involved in warfare activities, they could be deployed to create such systems.

A climate of peace would in itself enhance international cooperation for protecting the environment. For example, disputes over water in the Middle East are usually settled the way most disputes between Israel and its neighbours are settled – by the 'law of vendetta': as you do to me, so it will be done back to you. The remarkable thing is, this law of vendetta has worked, in a sense, when it comes to protecting water supply systems. With rare exceptions, there has been de facto agreement that water facilities are not proper targets. Aeroplanes are blown up, bus stations are bombed and airports are machine-gunned, but there are no attacks on water facilities. Each country is too vulnerable itself to counter-strikes against its water facilities to tolerate attacks by any other country against Israeli water facilities.

When the Palestine Liberation Organisation (PLO) started its campaign around 1969–70, it began by attacking Israeli water facilities. The Israelis responded by bombing Jordan's East Ghor Canal and the Maqarin Dam. This led to what is still remembered in the Middle East as 'Black September', when Jordan put an end to these attacks by forcefully expelling the PLO from its territory in September 1970. Jordan's water supply was too important to be jeopardised by PLO politicking.

How soil erosion can destroy a civilisation

The Mayan people developed and expanded steadily over seventeen centuries in the lowlands of Guatemala in Central America. Doubling on average every 408 years, the population had reached 5 million by AD900, with a density comparable to that of the most agriculturally intensive societies of today. At this peak – the highest level of civilisation agriculturally, culturally and architecturally – the Mayan world suddenly collapsed. Within a few decades the population fell to less than one-tenth of what it had been.

The reason was soil erosion; the Mayan people had destroyed the environmental foundation their advanced civilisation was based on.

The Mayans probably never grasped what brought their civilisation to a state of collapse. However many armies or weapons they may have had, these could never have stopped their downfall once their natural environment was destroyed.

36

❓ What are 'green taxes'?

Over the years, governments have insisted that corporations bear more of the cost of their own pollution. Green taxes would take this process further, enabling a government to use taxation to influence consumer and corporation behaviour.

During the past three decades, western governments have generally preferred legal codes over taxation systems for addressing environmental problems. They've introduced increasingly tougher environmental legislation, with widespread public support. Indeed, the legislation has become tougher irrespective of the political party in power; there is a momentum for change building that politicians can't afford to ignore. But governments haven't exploited the market approaches to their full potential: they haven't used the taxation system to make sure that polluters pay. Legislation, while useful, can't solve all the environmental problems. The law is always a blunt instrument, no matter where it is used, and tougher laws alone won't save the environment. For example, it isn't enough to ban the dumping of waste; there has to be an incentive to reuse the waste. 'Pollution' is simply a valuable resource in the wrong place.

Most local and national environmental legislation over the centuries has been concerned with 'end of the pipe' legislation – that is, stopping pollution, rather than changing how people live so that less pollution is produced in the first place.

Governments have been reluctant to make producers and consumers pay the full environmental cost of their activities. For example, the motor car is a very expensive mode of transport when the full cost is included. In the United States, for instance, the full cost – including the value of time wasted in traffic jams, the decline of property values near roads because of the noise, the cost of financing a formidable military presence in the Middle East, of combating lung disease and fending off global warming – totals at least US$350 billion a year. This is rarely acknowledged by industry, or by governments.

Recycling schemes are fine, but the real issue is whether the products should have been made in the first place. If we are going to save our environment we need to work towards reducing individual consumption levels, reducing dependence on fossil fuel, reducing the need for transportation of people and goods, and achieving a higher level of local production to meet local needs. Given the growing seriousness of environmental problems, governments will soon recognise that the market system can be used to protect the environment. This new approach will entail a paradigm shift among environmental activists, who have held economic growth and the market system responsible for many of the environmental problems in the first place.

Most taxation is policy-neutral, with the intention of simply raising revenue for the government, but taxation can also be used to help protect the environment. Most current taxation systems don't tell the ecological truth: that is, the taxes don't reflect the true costs of using resources. Governments could use green taxes to make sure that polluters pay the full cost of the harm they do – and so give them an incentive to operate more efficiently and cleanly.

The technical term is 'internalising the cost of production'. Many costs get 'externalised': the cost of water and air pollution, for example, is borne by the community. The eventual aim of green taxes will be to build the full cost of production into pricing, so the price of a product or service will incorporate its environmental cost. The intention isn't to add to the total cost of production, but to provide an incentive to look for cheaper forms of production. Competition in the marketplace shouldn't be between one corporation that's ruining the environment and another that's trying to save it. Competition should be between corporations that can do the best job in protecting the environment.

Here are some examples of how a green taxation could work. In essence, they come in four categories (not in any order of priority):

1. Increased taxation on certain activities that harm the environment.
2. The reduction (or elimination) of subsidies on activities that harm the environment.
3. The creation (or expansion) of taxation incentives to encourage activities that help the environment.
4. The creation (or expansion) of subsidies to encourage activities that help the environment.
   These might include:
   - increased taxes on the cost of cars – with taxation incentives given to the most environmentally safe

models; for example, the new hybrid-electric models
- increased taxation on petrol
- a tax on car-parking spaces in business districts to penalise the continued use of petrol
- taxes imposed on the first-time use of renewable resources, but reduced taxation on the use of recycled materials
- reducing subsidies for coal mining (Germany is a prime example of a country where each tonne of coal is subsidised by the government)
- abolishing environmentally damaging agricultural subsidies and applying a tax on chemical use in the agricultural sector to reduce the agricultural run-off of nutrients and chemicals
- providing financial assistance to financially disadvantaged people to improve the heating/cooling/insulation of their homes so that they use less energy
- allowing households to develop their own alternative ways of generating electricity and selling that electricity back to the grid system
- giving corporations tax incentives to encourage the research and development of alternative energy sources, such as wind power, small-scale hydro power, solar energy cells, geothermal and biomass power plants
- giving households tax incentives to use alternative energy sources
- subsidies to encourage the use of public transportation systems
- subsidies for 'retro-fitting' old buildings and old manufacturing equipment to make them more energy efficient.

37

❓ Who owns the South Pole?

The Antarctic is an entire continent controlled by a group of countries that have often disagreed among themselves elsewhere on the planet, especially the US and the Soviet Union and their respective allies.

The continent has never been colonised. Its isolation from Europe meant it wasn't on the list of potential targets for most of the time that Europeans were 'discovering' and 'claiming' other parts of the globe. Captain Cook is assumed to be the first European to sail close to the South Pole, but the rough Antarctic and Southern Oceans deterred further exploration south. Antarctica also wasn't involved in the later scramble for empire, when the 'unclaimed' parts of the globe had gone and the European powers were seeking to snatch the colonies of other European powers – a process that culminated in World Wars I and II. Antarctica was the only continent spared any military involvement in those conflicts.

Antarctica was spared because its inhospitable climate made permanent human settlement there impossible. Antarctica is the world's coldest, windiest and iciest continent. It's also the world's cleanest continent: diseases and humans have difficulty surviving in the cold.

The Antarctic is bigger than Europe west of the Urals or the mainland US. Its landmass is covered by ice up to 4 kilometres thick, and only about 3 per cent of the land is ice-free all year round. Antarctic ice represents about 80 per cent of the world's freshwater. The ice is an archive of the planet's history: sample cores of ice taken by scientists contain trapped bubbles of air that indicate climatic conditions on Earth during the past 150,000 years.

Humans first saw the ice near the continent about two centuries ago, but it required greatly improved technology before humans could reach the continent itself and live on it. Each year, Antarctica has about 3000 scientists resident in summer and about 800 in winter.

In the past, various countries have made claims to parts of the Antarctic. From about the 1820s, explorers from several countries landed there but none established a permanent presence. By the 1930s, seven countries had staked out claims: the UK, France, Australia, New Zealand and Norway – which recognised each other's claims – and Argentina and Chile, whose claims overlapped each other and with that of the UK. The largest single claimant was Australia, seeking rights to about 41 per cent of the continent – an area about the same size as continental Australia minus Queensland. At one point it was even considering claiming all of the continent, but the Norwegians had got in first.

1957–58 was the International Geophysical Year (IGY). It came at the height of US–Soviet Union political tensions, but there was no 'cold war' at the South Pole. Scientific activities took place in Antarctica, and the participating scientists from twelve countries knew that they had to cooperate or perish separately. Away from international political differences, the scientists were able to operate as a true fellowship of researchers. The success of IGY encouraged hopes of making the spirit of scientific cooperation more permanent, and in 1959 this was achieved through the Antarctic Treaty.

The 1959 Antarctic Treaty has five main strengths:

1. It has frozen all quarrels over claims. Under the treaty, no new claims may be made and those that have already been made canot be overturned. This is important given the nationalist fervour generated by the competing claims made by Argentina and Chile. Both countries have taken pregnant women to their claims – located on the only rock that is ice-free all year round – to have their babies born there. But these events have been seen simply as political gimmicks with no international legal significance. Despite this political pantomime, the treaty process has managed to keep a lid on excitable passions and there have been no wars. During the 1982 Falklands–Malvinas conflict, for example, the UK and Argentina maintained tranquil relations over Antarctic affairs, despite being enemies to the north.

2. It created the world's first nuclear-weapon free zone. Though perhaps only a minor breakthrough in itself in terms of limiting the arms race, it has been a helpful precedent for establishing more ambitious nuclear-free zones, notably the Moon, the seabed, Latin America,

the South Pacific and, most recently, Africa. It also helped the momentum for negotiations on international arms control.

3. The treaty was unusual for its time in that it created some form of international machinery. Many countries are willing to accept international obligations (via treaties), yet want to reserve to themselves the responsibility of ensuring that they keep their obligations; they're reluctant for any international interference in their domestic affairs. The Antarctic Treaty, however, by its consultative arrangements and mutual obligations, has created a limited international system of enforcement. The success of this treaty has encouraged later treaties on other matters to be gradually more ambitious.

4. The test of any international agreement is whether it is fulfilling its aims. The Antarctic Treaty certainly is. The memoirs of scientists who have worked in the Antarctic during the past five decades all attest to international cooperation. During the dark days of the Cold War, the level of cooperation in the Antarctic was virtually unequalled anywhere else in the world. Even when Australia severed its diplomatic relations with the Soviet Union during the 1960s over a spy scandal in Canberra, Russian and Australian scientists were working together in Antarctica. Political issues come and go, but scientific challenges remain and are often far more important in the long run.

5. The Antarctic Treaty is a showpiece of international law in operation. The treaty is self-enforcing: it's in each country's interest not to violate it because the gains from respecting the treaty's provisions far outweigh the gains that might result from breaking them.

The Antarctic Treaty has provided a good basis for other treaties. In 1972, the Convention for the Conservation of Antarctic Seals enforced the protection of some seal species and put controls on the catches of other seal species. No commercial sealing has been undertaken since the Convention came into force.

The 1980 Convention on the Conservation of Antarctic Marine Living Resources (CCAMLR) was negotiated in response to large-scale trawling for fin fish and krill (shrimp-like creatures) during the 1960s and 1970s, particularly by the USSR. This Convention represented a major break-through in marine conservation at the time, because, instead of considering each species separately, it provided for an 'eco-system as a whole' approach to conservation and marine resources. For example, whaling in Antarctic waters was banned by a separate body (the International Whaling Commission) but it would be pointless to save the whales from being hunted when they could, in theory, starve to death because their food, the krill, had been caught by trawlers.

With CCAMLR completed, the Antarctic Treaty Consultative Parties turned their attention to the need to regulate mining and oil drilling. But this coincided with speculation that Antarctica could become the scene of an oil, natural gas and mineral rush because some transnational corporations had hopes of exploiting the continent's wealth. Environmental non-government organisations, loosely coordinated by the Antarctic and South Oceans Coalition, fought that proposal throughout the 1980s. Eventually, public opinion swung round to their point of view and they achieved one of the greatest environmental victories of the decade (see 'How environmental NGOs beat governments'), forcing the Antarctic Treaty Consultative Parties to stop all dreams of mineral prospecting and oil drilling. Instead, a treaty to ban all such prospecting and drilling came into being: the Environmental Protocol.

The Environmental Protocol was signed in 1991 and entered into effect in 1998 – Australia is one of the countries that has ratified it. The protocol bans mining for at least fifty years and, with its establishment of high standards for all human activities on the continent, goes a long way towards safeguarding Antarctica before it suffers from the human impacts felt over most of the rest of the planet.

Antarctica is the world's last great wilderness, a continent of remarkable beauty and a vital international scientific laboratory. The Environmental Protocol helps solidify its location as one of the most significant areas for international scientific cooperation. For a continent with competing claimants, Antarctica has brought out the best of human qualities rather than the worst, but it's a 'good news' story and so is consistently overlooked by the mass media.

How environmental NGOs beat governments

Throughout the 1980s, a number of NGOs – loosely coordinated by the Antarctic and South Oceans Coalition (ASOC), which brought together over 200 NGOs in forty-five countries – fought the proposed treaty to regulate mining in Antarctica: the Convention for the Regulation of Antarctic Mineral Resource Activities (CRAMRA).

We argued that it was wrong even to speculate that mining or drilling for oil or natural gas could be a possibility in Antarctica, and so it was wrong to devote any attention to drafting a treaty to regulate such activities. Our view was that there should be a complete ban on mining and drilling for oil and natural gas. An accidental oil slick would take much longer to biodegrade in the cold climate of the Antarctic than in the warmer climate of, say, the Middle East.

For many years it seemed a forlorn struggle for the NGOs, with the Consultative Parties progressing, albeit at a slow pace, towards a treaty. The Convention for the Regulation of Antarctic Mineral Resource Activities was opened for signature on 25 November 1988, but it never came into force. The demise of CRAMRA is one of the greatest environmental victories of that decade.

Environmental NGOs forced the Antarctic Treaty Consultative Parties to stop all work on mineral prospecting and oil drilling, and instead create a treaty to ban all such prospecting and drilling. This success was due to a mixture of skilful environmental activism, renewed media attention on environmental problems, and ambitious politicians in some of the Consultative Parties who were anxious to respond to the public's heightened awareness of environmental issues.

The environmental problems included scientific speculations over the so-called 'greenhouse effect' and the hole in the ozone layer over Antarctica. These coincided with a very hot summer and extensive bushfires in the US, which were unrelated but which the mass media found newsworthy. Additionally, in March 1989, the *Exxon Valdez* oil tanker — captained by a man who was banned from driving a car because of drunkenness but was still allowed to run a ship — ran aground in Alaska and created what was then the largest oil slick in US history (about the size of the state of Delaware). This was exactly the type of disaster NGOs had warned could happen if oil drilling were carried out in Antarctica.

Meanwhile, politicians were looking for ways to prove they were 'green' to match this new level of environmental concern. In Australia, with an election looming, the Leader of the Opposition, John Howard, suddenly spoke out against CRAMRA. He'd worked out where the crowd was heading and so ran in front of it claiming to be its leader. Those of us involved in the campaign hadn't previously known of his interest in Antarctic matters, but we welcomed his sudden conversion. The Australian Government decided equally suddenly to disown its work on CRAMRA. A similar form of politicking was under way in France and the French Government made the same decision around that time.

Having spent so long creating CRAMRA, the Consultative Parties then quickly got to work on a ban on mining in Antarctica – which had been the NGOs' argument all along. The ensuing Madrid Protocol entered into force in 1998.

This case study shows how effective NGOs can be in overcoming governments.

38

❓ Can democracy be exported?

The growth of democracy was one of the positive pieces of news in the twentieth century. In 1900 not a single country had what we would today consider a democracy: a government created by elections in which every adult citizen could vote. Those countries that had elections often restricted the voting to white men, and in some countries the men also had to be property owners. Australia and New Zealand led the world in pioneering votes for women.

Today, 119 out of the 191 UN member-states are democracies, which means that about 62 per cent of the world's people live in a democracy and that it has gone from being a form of government to a way of life. 'Democracy' is Greek for 'the rule of the people', but ironically Classical Greece wasn't a democracy because only property-owning men were allowed to vote.

However, as the people of Iraq are now learning – there's more to a democracy than just voting. There has to be the creation of a set of social values to underpin the process, which doesn't happen overnight. A fully democratic society includes:

- respect for the rule of law
- an independent judiciary
- separation of religious and secular authority
- civilian control of the military
- respect for human rights such as assembly, property and belief.

Britain and the US are seen as among the pioneers that spread the democratic process around the world, but it took centuries to evolve in those countries. Before the Reform Act in Britain in 1832, only 1.8 per cent of the population voted. After the change of law, the figure rose to 2.7 per cent but was still limited to property-owning white males. The electorate was widened again in 1867, to 6.4 per cent; and in 1884 to 12.1 per cent. Women got the vote after World War I. The principle of one person–one vote wasn't fully established until after World War II, when students at Oxford and Cambridge universities no longer got two votes: one at home and one in their university constituency.

The US's history isn't much better. For the first few decades after the founding of the US in 1776, only white male property owners could vote. The US had rebelled against King George III's dictatorship but it still copied Britain's elite system of voting. In 1824 – forty-eight years after independence – still only 5 per cent of adult Americans could vote in a presidential election, none of them women or slaves. Black Americans got the vote – in theory – after the Civil War

(1861–65), but in fact many states in the South didn't give their black population a free vote until a century later. American women got the vote in 1920.

Ironically, throughout all this time Britain and the US held themselves up as the models of democracy to be followed by the rest of the world. The British also took their views into their empire, but they had mixed success. Many of the democratic countries created by Britain in the decolonisation process later fell into dictatorships, especially in Africa. The success stories are Australia, Canada, India and New Zealand.

No parliamentary 'seats' for Australian women

Australia was one of the world's first countries to give women the vote, but it didn't occur to many Australians – male or female – that this meant women could actually get elected to Parliament. Old Parliament House, built in the 1920s, had no toilets for female politicians; the men who worked out the original building specifications couldn't imagine there'd ever be any need for them, even though the specifications were drawn up about two decades after women first got the vote.

As recently as three decades ago, few would have predicted the current tidal wave of democracy sweeping the world – across Eastern Europe, Taiwan, the Philippines, South Korea, Indonesia. People power is making itself felt. Dictatorial leaders have a dilemma: if they want rapid economic development, they run the risk of being deposed by the very beneficiaries of their policies.

So how is it happening? The key factors are domestic economic growth and globalisation.

Domestic economic growth

A brutal dictatorship can run a poor peasant society based on agriculture, because poor peasants living on isolated farms in desolate valleys or plains don't make good revolutionaries. They're too worried about the perils of daily survival. A peasant society has a poverty consciousness: it's poor and expects to remain that way. It doesn't like the poverty but can see little opportunity to escape.

But a dictatorship can't run a modern industrial state, because this requires the free flow of people, money, information and ideas. You can't design computers with bayonets. Economic development creates a middle class, which is urban-based, well-educated and able to learn – via the mass media, internet and overseas travel – about how other societies are governed. The free flow of information enables people to discuss not only technical matters, such as computer design, but also wider social and political issues.

The rising middle class causes huge problems for a dictator. They get a little money and then they want more; they have rising expectations. The richer they get, the more politically restive they become. They can see that change is possible and they want a say in how they're being governed. They feel empowered about their destiny and are less deferential to the ruling elite. The growing middle class aren't as willing to accept that certain people are born to rule or should have special inherited privileges. They prefer people to earn their status by merit, not just by birth. When the belly is full, the brain starts to think.

People power is enshrined in non-governmental organisations (NGOs). There are thousands of NGOs in each developed western country, such as the women's movement, student organisations, human rights, peace and environment movements. NGOs provide an alternative opportunity for involvement in public affairs in democratic societies. They're also the main vehicle for opposition to dictatorial regimes in developing countries. NGOs have led the struggle to depose dictators.

Ironically, dictators often create their own problems by encouraging economic growth. This happened in Indonesia in the 1990s: when Suharto plugged the country into the global economy, Indonesians weren't satisfied with just economic growth – they eventually wanted a say in how the country was being governed. They could see how other people lived overseas and they too wanted the good things of life. They assumed that if Indonesia were a democracy, there would be more freedom of opinion, more accountability and political transparency, less corruption and police brutality, and more economic growth.

The effect of globalisation on repression

There seems to be a descending scale of repression in many countries. Not every leader today has the stomach of Pol Pot for the mass murder of their perceived opponents. The USSR is the best example. Stalin was last century's largest mass murderer, but his successors were less violent towards their critics. For example, in the 1956 Hungarian uprising, government leader Imre Nagy was killed and his body was thrown into a mass grave. However in the 'Prague Spring' of 1968, the reformist Alexander Dubček was moved sideways into a minor public service job instead of being assassinated. This meant that when Czechoslovakia's 'Velvet Revolution' took place at the end of the 1980s, he was still around to take up a senior parliamentary position in the new democracy.

The international mass media have made it more difficult for dictators today to control unruly student and middle-class activists. Suharto and the military came to power in Indonesia in the mid-1960s amid a civil war in which at least 500,000 people (possibly a million) were killed. But Suharto couldn't use the same brutal tactics when he was under threat in the 1990s because the whole world was watching.

The US overlooked the military's massacre in Indonesia in the 1960s because it hoped that a more pro-US regime would come to power. This was the time of the Cold War, and the US looked at all human rights issues in relation to the need to oppose the Soviet Union. By the late 1990s, the Soviet Union was long gone and so human rights issues were more often examined on their own merits. By now, the US no longer needed Suharto.

I was in Manila, the Philippines, in January 1986 during the people power revolution and saw first-hand how the corrupt Marcos regime was hindered from using brute force by the risk of adverse international mass media coverage. Governments may be able to control their own media, but they can't control the foreign media or their citizens' ability to get access to foreign media coverage.

Finally, a modern industrial state is interconnected with the global economy. A harshly repressive regime is bad for a country's business image and can scare off foreign investment. Business leaders may have some loyalty to their own country and government, but they also have to think about the bottom line: violence is bad for business. Political leaders come and go but business goes on. In the Philippines, the Manila business community decided that Marcos was bad for foreign investment and so he had to go.

Where will we see civil unrest next? Probably in China, whose old men seem to have forgotten their Marxism. Marx claimed that economic changes inevitably bring about political changes. We saw this played out in the Soviet Union, with Gorbachev's attempt to encourage both economic change and political reform. He hoped to control the political reform while the economic change took place; instead, of course, Gorbachev was swept away by the political reforms. But China's old men want economic reform while keeping the Communist Party in power; they're foolishly ignoring the advice from Marx and the lessons of history. The really big domino has yet to fall. The problem for the rest of the world is that China's economic growth is now important for many people overseas. An upheaval in China threatens the global economy.

39

Can democracy take root in Arab societies?

Arab countries, and Iran, stand in stark contrast to the rest of the world, where freedom and democracy have been gaining ground over the past two decades. The Arab League has twenty-two members and not one is a democracy as the term is defined in western countries – though the US hopes that Iraq will become a functioning democracy.

Arab rulers are corrupt and heavy-handed. Almost every Arab country today is less free than it was forty years ago. The reason is oil wealth – it's transformed the Arab desert kingdoms for the worse. Before all that money came along, the rulers could only rule in a relaxed fashion. They were poor and had little power; their people were nomadic which made it difficult to control and tax them; and the rulers couldn't afford large military or police forces.

But then the oil wealth started to pour in. Now the rulers can afford large military forces (Arab countries are among the world's best customers for international arms dealers) and so they can put down political opposition. They don't have any electoral accountability. Rich rulers don't need to tax their people, and if the citizens aren't being taxed, why should they have a say in how the country is being governed? Arab rulers ask little of their people – and, in return, give little to them.

But Arab rulers are mostly less corrupt and heavy-handed than the fanatical Islamic groups that want to replace them. Osama bin Laden claims that Arab countries aren't Islamic enough. He sees democracy as a western trick to erode Islamic religious values. This attitude makes it difficult for Arab rulers to get reforms adopted. In 2003, for example, the US encouraged Kuwait – which it had liberated from Saddam Hussein's Iraq in 1991 – to give women the vote. But the Kuwaiti Parliament, dominated by Islamic fundamentalists, rejected the idea.

Saudi Crown Prince Abdullah proposed a less dramatic idea: that women in his country should be allowed to drive a car. This was also blocked by Islamic fundamentalists – which means Saudi Arabia has to import half a million chauffeurs from places like India and the Philippines.

But is Islam always a block to democracy? Not at all. There's no automatic reason to think that democracy couldn't eventually take root in Arab societies.

For instance, most Muslims now live outside Arab countries. There are 1.2 billion Muslims in total, but only 260 million live in the Arab world. Many live in democracies, such as Australia, the UK, India and the US, and are involved in the democratic process. If there is a fundamental contradiction between Islam and democracy, it's not apparent to about 800 million Muslims.

Indonesia is the world's most populous Islamic country, and has immense problems, not least with corruption, but it's giving democracy a go. Turkey, which has the world's fifth-largest Islamic population, is also a democracy. It too has many problems, not least with the political power of its military, but it's an American ally in the North Atlantic Treaty Organization (NATO) and is hoping to join the European Union.

Islam itself isn't necessarily a religion of repression and backwardness. There is much in the Koran that talks about the need to respect strong rulers, but similar traditional views can also be found in the Bible. In Russia, the tsar was considered almost a god; the emperor in Japan *was* a god. But traditional societies can change, as we've seen in both those countries. In fact, Islam has a tradition of opposing cruel dictators. Muslims are required to obey the ruler – provided the ruler follows God's laws. Otherwise they have a right to rebellion against unjust rulers. In 1776, the Americans used similar reasoning to rebel against King George III. It may yet be possible for Arab societies to become democracies.

40

? Will the US succeed in making Iraq a democracy?

The world has more democracies than ever before, but they are home-grown; they haven't been imposed from the outside. This suggests that the American dream of exporting democracy to Iraq is doomed to failure.

Personally, I doubt the US will be able to inject democracy into Iraq. The Iraqis very bravely defied the violence and got out to vote in January 2005, but there's more to democracy than just holding an election. When the British left their colonies in Africa, for example, they usually arranged for an election, but most of those colonies soon fell into dictatorships. It will take some years to see what flows from the 2005 election in Iraq.

Iraqis need to work things out for themselves, which may take decades, not merely years. After all, democracy didn't suddenly occur in the UK or US – it evolved over centuries. In the meantime, Iraq needs economic growth and the recreation of the middle class – which was destroyed by the US's sanctions against Iraq during the 1990s.

With the benefit of hindsight, perhaps an alternative grand strategy for the US in the 1990s would have been to ease up on the sanctions, allow economic growth to take place, enable the middle class to grow – and then let political events take their own course domestically. Given that the tidal wave of democracy has eventually swept away even brutal dictators like Suharto in Indonesia, could this process have worked in Iraq in the 1990s, leading to the fall of Saddam Hussein? This is an intriguing question that will never be answered.

Democracy can triumph. But it has to come from within the country, in its own time.

41

❓ Is foreign aid a waste of money?

Not necessarily – though some of it could be better spent.

Foreign aid is part of one of the greatest projects in the second half of the twentieth century: where developed countries try to help developing counties to become developed. The project continues to this day. It means achieving in a few decades what some countries (such as the UK and US) took centuries to achieve.

When people think of the harsh way of life in developing countries today and despair of economic progress ever being achieved, it's worth recalling that life was also harsh in many developed countries in past decades. For example, in 1914, only 40 per cent of British recruits in World War I were physically fit for military service. By the time World War II began in 1939, the percentage hadn't improved by much. There's been an improvement in the ordinary physical lives of Britons in recent decades, however, and there's no inherent reason why such an improvement couldn't also be achieved in Africa and Asia in the future.

Just sixty years ago almost all these developing countries were still colonies. Only two countries in Africa have no recent history of colonisation: Liberia and Ethiopia; and two countries in Asia: Japan and Thailand. All of North, Central and Latin America have been colonised.

The development process for most developing countries has been difficult – but, then, it wasn't easy for the UK or US either. While much favourable publicity is given to the newly industrialised countries (NICs), especially in East Asia, most developing countries haven't achieved the targets laid down in the UN Development Decades, which began forty-five years ago.

Indeed, in some African countries people were economically better off under their European colonial rulers. In the early years of the decolonisation process, such countries could claim they were still subjects of neocolonialism, with their former colonial masters still running their economies. Robert Mugabe of Zimbabwe, for example, has been fond of using this explanation for his country's continued slide into political and economic chaos. But the further these countries get from their date of independence, the less that form of blaming has relevance. Robert Mugabe has destroyed his country by taking land from white settlers and giving it to his cronies instead of redistributing the land to people who used to work on it and so know something about farming. Zimbabwe, a 'bread basket' of Africa, is now having to rely on food aid.

Obstacles to development

There are various domestic obstacles to development. Poor countries remain poor partly because they lack money for investment. There is a capital shortage to sustain large investments in infrastructure – such as transport, education, health services and developing new sources of energy – and the creation of new industries. Developing countries are supplied with some foreign aid to help with establishing infrastructure.

Developing countries lack scientific and technological research and development facilities: 97 per cent of all the world's scientists are located in the developed western and former Communist nations. That means 80 per cent of humankind have only 3 per cent of the world's scientists. Even if developing countries receive sophisticated equipment as part of their foreign aid programs, there's no guarantee that they will be able to make the most of it as there's a shortage of skilled personnel to run complicated equipment.

There's also a lack of entrepreneurial skills. Business 'get up and go' is taken for granted in developed countries, but it takes a while for an entrepreneurial culture to evolve.

Foreign aid is important, but it is not the only key factor in improving life in developing countries. Many poor nations are still devoting a great deal of attention – in terms of money and skilled personnel – to running defence forces. It's shocking to see how these countries maintain their own poverty partly by being involved in conflicts.

Finally, many developing countries have corrupt rulers, who acquire foreign aid funds and use them for their own purposes rather than for national development. Some transnational corporations won't invest in corrupt developing countries because of the need to pay bribes on a continuing basis to get anything done. Transnational corporations aren't going to risk their investments and their foreign-recruited staff in such countries.

The importance of trade

It makes no sense trying to bring about the development of developing countries, to allow them to build up their manufacturing capacities and expand the production of their goods and services, and then deny them access to a foreign developed market where they can sell them.

Foreign aid could be a bridge to nowhere unless developing countries are given access to foreign technology and foreign markets. This means allowing them to export their textiles and foodstuffs into developed countries. This is potentially very controversial because local farmers and producers may lose out. But it's good news for local consumers because it will offer them a greater variety of goods at a lower price.

'Ruined for life'

I've been involved in development issues for forty years. Being aware of the problems of countries in Africa and Asia at an early age has given me a different perception of the world. It's hard to take seriously many of the concerns in British or Australian life when you know the everyday trials faced by a person living in developing countries. In the midst of global abundance, about 1.1 billion people live on less than US$1 per day. Our problems in Australia are minute by comparison, but we lead such self-absorbed and self-indulgent lives that we're unaware of many of the problems of most of humanity.

Father Pete Henriot, an American Jesuit priest now based in Africa, warned some young Americans that if they did voluntary service in Africa or Asia they would be 'ruined for life'. Having served in a poor country and then returned home to the affluence of the US, they'd be shocked by how irrelevant many of the American everyday issues seemed.

I realise that I too have been 'ruined for life'. What I've seen in developing countries haunts me. I have difficulty in taking many Australian 'problems' really seriously – compared, say, with the plight of a person in an African or Asian country who spends about two hours a day simply looking for water and firewood to survive.

Charity begins at home

There's a lot of ignorance in Australia about foreign aid, and international affairs generally. I'm in favour of more foreign aid being spent *in* Australia to build up a climate of support for foreign aid. Grants could be made to non-government organisations to operate educational programs, as NGOs are more successful than government bureaucrats at running campaigns – and much less expensive in their operating costs.

Forty years ago, the United Nations agreed that countries should give 0.7 per cent of their gross national product (GNP) for foreign aid. Australia – like many western countries – is now giving the least amount of aid since records began. But there's little political outrage about this. Indeed, Australian foreign ministers over the years have pointed out that what few letters they do get on foreign aid are usually in favour of cutting it rather than expanding it.

It's interesting to note that the countries that meet or exceed the UN target – they're all in Scandinavia – are also those that have run domestic educational campaigns. Giving foreign aid and being a good international citizen are seen as part of the national identity of these countries. Changes in political parties in power make no difference. Australia should be aiming to achieve a similar way of thinking.

42

Is Islam a threat to world peace?

The September 11 attacks on New York and Washington DC, the 2001 conflict in Afghanistan, the 2003 conflict in Iraq, and the bomb attacks on tourist destinations, such as Bali and London, have all fuelled speculation that Islam is a threat to world peace. Fundamentalist Islam is a great problem within some societies, but it's not necessarily a threat to international peace and security.

It's true that Islam is on the rise again, but the 'Islamic world' is not a united monolithic bloc and Islam is therefore not necessarily a military threat to western countries.

The three phases of Islam

Islam has gone through three major phases. The first phase (622–1683) saw the expansion of the faith from Saudi Arabia, west across northern Africa and east to Indonesia. It reached Europe through Spain and almost took over Vienna in 1683. This period included the successful Islamic defence of the Holy Land against the European Crusaders of the Middle Ages.

A thousand years ago, the best educated and most scientifically advanced lands in the western hemisphere were under Islamic control; the major advances in science, astronomy and medicine at that time came from the Arab world. To this day we still use Arabic figures (1, 2, 3 . . .) as the basis of numbers, and coffee is an Arab invention.

In the second phase (1683–1945) the west – having stopped the spread of Islam at Vienna – counter-attacked and colonised many Islamic lands; the defeats of the Crusades were avenged. During this time, Britain's Queen Victoria controlled more Muslims than any other ruler in history – in the Indian subcontinent (present-day India, Pakistan and Bangladesh) and across northern and eastern Africa.

The European colonial expansion bypassed the Islamic-controlled Middle East. In 1492, Christopher Columbus sailed to what are now the Americas in search of an alternative sea-based trade route to Asia, as the overland Silk Road route – now Muslim territory – was no longer possible. With the loss of international trade, the Arab world became a backwater and the people lost their thirst for knowledge and respect for education. Instead, the Europeans became the world leaders in knowledge.

The rise of the European nation-state system (the Westphalian System) was also a blow to the Islamic world. Islam speaks of the oneness of God, and Muslims see themselves as a global community, but this unity is hindered by the political reality of separate nation-states.

In the current phase, beginning in about 1945, there has been a resurgence of Islam; it's now one of the world's fastest-growing religions. Muslims today represent about 18.5 per cent of the world's population, and Islam is the second-largest religious group after Christianity. London has become one of the 'capitals' of the Islamic world, as different Islamic groups can meet there in an atmosphere of neutrality and safety, whereas they may not be so welcome in each other's country.

A religion can grow by 'conversion', such as Christian evangelists preaching the message to convert agnostics or atheists to Christianity. It can encourage people of one faith to change to its own version. Or it can grow biologically, by encouraging parents, as part of their religious duty, to have several children and raise those children in the faith. The resurgence of Islam is particularly based on biological growth, hence the large size of many Islamic families.

Why Islam is not necessarily a military threat to the west

First of all, the 'Islamic world' is not a united monolithic bloc. One lesson the west learned from the Cold War was that the 'Communist bloc' was never really the homogeneous entity stretching from Berlin to Beijing that some politicians claimed it to be. The Eastern European countries resented the Soviet occupation, the Soviet Asian Republics resented the (Communist) Russian occupation, and the USSR and China were never on good terms. Old nationalisms, historical grudges, racism and various other less pleasant aspects of human nature can all erode any form of global religion. We mustn't assume that Islam is a more unifying force than any other religion or political ideology.

When the British left India in 1947, they were forced by Islamic leaders to divide the empire into India and Pakistan, as the Muslims wanted their own Islamic homeland. Pakistan then consisted of West Pakistan and East Pakistan, on either side of northern India. When it was pointed out that there was no common land corridor uniting both halves, the British expert drawing up the boundary said their common religion would hold the country together. It didn't. East Pakistan broke away during the 1971 civil war to create the separate country of Bangladesh, proving that Islam itself is not necessarily a unifying factor.

Second, Islam has long been a divided religion. The split between the Sunnis (about 800 million) and the Shi'as (about 110 million) began in AD632, with the death of the prophet Mohammed. The Sunnis claim that the prophet wanted his successors to be chosen by consensus, whereas the Shi'as claim that he wanted the leaders chosen only from within his family line. The Shi'as have a highly organised clergy and a strict hierarchical system of interpreting God's will on earth (much like the Catholic Church). The Sunnis have no central ecclesiastical authority and are fragmented (like the various Protestant denominations).

During the Afghanistan civil war throughout the 1990s, Iran supported the embattled Shi'as based in the north, while Pakistan and the US supported the Pathan Taliban movement – which, ironically, was notorious for keeping women at home, banning drugs and hanging smashed televisions from trees. The Taliban also hosted Osama bin Laden's al-Qai'da network.

Many Muslim populations are spread around the world, from North Africa on the Atlantic coast across to Indonesia. The Arab world, in population terms, is only a small percentage of the Islamic population worldwide; Muslims are, in fact, present in most countries. They're a major ethnic minority in western China, for example; and there are also Danish Muslims, Scottish Muslims and American Muslims.

The latter will soon outnumber American Jews, and have already outnumbered the Episcopalian Christians (who have provided many American presidents). Islam will soon become the largest non-Christian faith in the US. This will have interesting implications for the US's Middle East policy, because a large slice of the young service personnel will be Islamic: how will they feel serving a government so committed to defending Israel?

Meanwhile, the Koran isn't an easy book to read: it's unclear in about 20 per cent of the text. Even in Arabic – its official language – there are passages that modern scholars can't work out. This kind of difficulty helps explain the various different interpretations of the Koran, such as the meaning of the word 'jihad', for example.

It also leads to differences of opinion over the application of strict Islamic law, such as stoning to death. Indonesia – the world's most populous Islamic country – has many easygoing Muslims who don't want strict Islamic law. Similarly, the Malaysian Government is well aware that its influx of foreign investment requires a more tolerant Islamic approach.

Finally, there's no agreed manifesto to unify Muslims against the west. The Koran isn't a recipe for waging wars against infidels. Apart from various degrees of hostility towards Israel, there are few issues that unite all Muslims.

The challenges of Islam for the west

Islam presents two challenges to the west. First, the west has to recognise the diversity and complexity of the Islamic world. There's more to the 'Islamic world' than just the militant Arab countries, Afghanistan, Iran, Egypt and Algeria. Indeed, most Muslims don't even live in the Arab world.

Take Kuwait in 1990–91, for example: many people in the west didn't realise just how hated the al-Sabah regime was in much of the Middle East. The Iraqi invasion of Kuwait was praised by many poor Arabs, but the west lined up with a fundamentalist dictatorship and was supported by another dictatorship in Saudi Arabia. This wasn't a crusade against Islam: Saddam Hussein was less fundamental in his beliefs than the countries the US supported. (Ironically, when the 1992 elections were held in Kuwait, women and stateless Arabs were still excluded from the poll.)

Second, we need to recognise the importance of history. There is still a deep-seated resentment at the west's violence towards Islam over the centuries. Many more Muslims have been killed by Christians, than Christians by Muslims. Countries that used to have colonies have tended to forget about their imperial pasts, but Muslims retain a deeper memory of being run by foreigners.

A by-product of the September 11 attacks has been the sudden revival of western interest in Islam. There are now probably more biographies on Mohammed available than at any other time in history. Some people want to know what it is about Islamic thinking that can encourage wealthy young men to take their own lives in terrorist attacks. The men who flew the planes into the World Trade Center weren't ignorant or poor; they had plenty of options ahead of them. They had everything to live for; yet, despite all their wealth, they looked for something else.

Others are interested to know what it is in Islamic thinking that gives such men such courage. They knew they were destined to die yet they went ahead with the operation. Much the same could be said of the suicide bombers in the Middle East, some of whom are women. In an age of global consumerism, when people are encouraged to believe that money can solve all problems, there are some for whom the promise of wealth isn't enough. Like Mohammed, they are turning their backs on wealth and seeking a different answer.

43

❓ What are the threats to Islam?

The west often focuses on the tensions between Islam and its own world, but we need to be aware that Islam has problems of its own, which come from within the religion itself.

Women's rights

Muslim women want more say. In Afghanistan, the Americans have been insisting that women play a greater role in how the country is governed, but this is clearly contrary to some of the traditional viewpoints of conservative Islamic leaders. (Ironically, thanks to American pressure, Afghanistan now has, in percentage terms, more national women politicians than there are in the US Congress or the Australian Parliament.) Some moderate Islamic countries actually have a better reputation than western countries for having women as rulers: Indonesia, Pakistan, Bangladesh and Turkey, for example. But other Islamic countries – such as those in the Arab world, and Iran – are appalled by the idea of allowing women such a high level of responsibility. Tough. The fact is, women are now demanding a greater role – and the old men who run conservative, medieval Islamic societies will be forced to cope with this.

Some of the Islamic leaders are being mugged by reality. Iran, for instance, was one of the world's best success stories in family planning. One of the first things the Ayatollah Khomeini did in 1979 when he came to power was to dismantle the family planning system established by the Shah of Iran. Instead, he advocated large families. Then Saddam Hussein attacked his country and so there was a need for a large army.

Now, Iran's religious leaders realise that having one of the world's fastest-growing populations is wrecking the country's economic prospects and straining its infrastructure. Mullahs who once were on the front lines urging women to have more children are now encouraging them to have fewer. Contraceptives are now available free of charge, and Iranian couples intending to get married are obliged to take a two-day course in family planning and contraception in order to get a marriage licence. If Iran, with its strong undercurrent of Islamic fundamentalism, can move so quickly towards population stability, there is hope for countries elsewhere.

In April 2005 it was reported that Saudi Arabia had banned forced marriage. The grand mufti, the country's highest religious leader, said that forced marriage was against Islamic teaching and those that continue with it should go to prison. The high rate of forced marriages is believed to be a factor in the country's steep divorce rate: about 50 per cent of marriages end in divorce.

Modern Muslim women can draw inspiration from a grand Islamic tradition of strong women. Khadija, the wife of the prophet Mohammed, was a rich woman (a widow with a merchant background) who actually proposed to him. When Mohammed began to receive his divine revelations of the new faith, she backed him with her wealth.

In the seventh century, Muslim Arab women were freer and had more rights than their sisters anywhere else in the world. They could divorce, inherit property and many were noted writers. They even led armies.

In India, the high point of the Islamic era came with the Mughals. The Taj Mahal, one of the world's most impressive buildings, was built to honour a seventeenth-century woman, Mumtaz Mahal. And for part of the seventeenth century, the empire was run by a woman, Nur Jehan, Empress of India.

There's continuing discussion on how Muslim women ended up in their current second-class status. This is not something specified in the Koran; given the role of his wife, the prophet could not have ordained such a lowly status for women. It seems that the problem occurred with the arrival of the European colonists. Muslim men put their women into seclusion mainly to protect them. This was their defensive response to the invasion, as women symbolised their honour and dignity.

Islamic women are now coming out of the home and into the world. They will have as much impact on the Islamic world as they've had on politics elsewhere.

Children's rights

Children in conservative Islamic societies are starting to demand consumer goods. Young people in most countries have similar tastes for pop music, clothes, and videos.

During my trips behind the Iron Curtain in the 1970s and 1980s, I noticed that the young people may have been militarily loyal to Moscow, but they wanted American fast food, jeans and soft drinks. It was this desire for western goods and services that helped erode the power of the old men who ran the Soviet Union.

The same process is happening now in the Islamic world. In Iran, for example, over half the population are aged under eighteen, and they're tired of the conservative old men who run the country. They want access to all the things western consumerism can promise. The September 11 terrorists turned their backs on the promise of wealth. They weren't taken in by global consumerism; in fact, they were possibly revolted by it. But many of their contemporaries feel differently.

Jobs and economic growth

The Islamic world has a rapidly growing population – it's a Muslim's duty to have many children and to raise them as Muslims. But there are no jobs for all those people.

Many Muslims in the Middle East and elsewhere are missing out on economic growth. Years ago, a lot of the leaders opposing governments in North Africa and the Middle East would have been Communist; now they are Islamic. Muslims have seen the collapse of the Soviet Union and its Eastern European allies; they've also derived little benefit from the quasi-socialistic regimes in places like Egypt, which are large, inefficient bureaucracies unable to cope with rapid urbanisation and population growth.

There's a great deal of resentment among people in the Islamic world that their life is a lot harsher than it is for those in the western world. Young people have access to the media and so they can see from foreign programs how well people live in western countries. The Muslims in the Middle East blame their leaders for their own lack of progress. They remember the dominant world-class status the Islamic world enjoyed centuries ago and they're angry that they're now so backward. They don't like living in a backwater.

A common mindset in Iraq now is: 'Americans go home – and take me with you.' People feel anger towards their corrupt and inefficient governments. In some countries, such as Algeria and Egypt, this anger has developed into low-intensity warfare.

In short, many Islamic countries have internal problems that result in violence within their own boundaries.

44

❓ What are 'human rights'?

Human rights are fundamental privileges or immunities to which all people have a claim. They're not 'given' by governments since they are derived automatically from being a human. Since governments can't 'give' human rights, they shouldn't try to take them away.

Human rights thinking – especially since 1945 – is based on the assumption that all human beings have a common core. They may be divided on gender lines, speak different languages and have different skin colours, but fundamentally there are great similarities between all humans. The 1945 United Nations Charter picks this up with such references as 'fundamental human rights', 'the dignity and worth of the human person', 'equal rights' and 'fundamental freedoms'.

What are 'human rights'?

The basic UN human rights document is the 1948 Universal Declaration of Human Rights. Its thirty Articles include:

- the right to life, liberty and security of person
- equality before the law
- freedom of movement and residence
- freedom from torture or cruel, inhuman or degrading treatment or punishment
- the right to seek in other nations asylum from persecution
- freedom of thought, religion and conscience
- the rights to vote and to participate in government
- the right to education
- the right to work
- the right to form and join trades unions
- the right to an adequate standard of living
- the right to health protection
- the right to participate fully in cultural life.

There are two general categories of human rights. Almost all human rights apply to individuals; but there is also one collective human right: the right to self-determination – that is, for a 'people' to run their own affairs. The collective right to self-determination has a long history, although the term itself is modern. For example, when Moses led the Hebrews out of Egypt, he was the leader (in our terms) of a 'national liberation movement' and the Hebrews were seeking 'self-determination'. George Washington, Ho Chi Minh and Nelson Mandela are more recent examples of leaders of peoples wishing to exercise their right of self-determination.

The category of individual human rights may be further divided into three subcategories. The oldest human rights are civil and political, such as the rights to a fair trial and to take part in politics. About a century ago, as European countries started to create 'welfare states', recognition was given to economic and social rights, such as the rights to work and to equal pay for equal work. The newest rights are more general ones, such as the rights to peace and to a healthy environment.

Human rights and 'internal affairs'

Human rights received considerable attention during the drafting of the 1945 UN Charter. Hitler had shown that a country that violates human rights at home may eventually violate human rights overseas, and so it was necessary to nip such threats in the bud. Also, the Allied countries were embarrassed that none of them had complained officially between 1933 (when Hitler came to power) and 1939 (the onset of World War II) about the treatment of Jews. They claimed during that period that countries weren't allowed to interfere in the internal affairs of other nations, which prohibited even the criticism of other countries' internal policies.

As discussed in 'Is globalisation good or bad', the Westphalian System of nation-states is based on 'national sovereignty'; that is, each country governs itself and can't be forced into accepting international obligations. Its 'internal' affairs remain internal and so a country can't be forced into accepting any international involvement in its human rights policies.

The UN Charter's Article 2 (7) rules out any UN involvement in matters 'which are essentially within the domestic jurisdiction' of any country. The use of the word 'essentially' was derived from other provisions of the UN Charter that noted the importance of human rights. By implication, these provisions foreshadowed some UN involvement in domestic human rights issues.

Article 2 (7) has been gradually eroded. For example, in the late 1940s, India raised at the UN General Assembly the racist policies of South Africa. South Africa claimed these couldn't be discussed because they were an internal matter under Article 2 (7) and managed to win that argument for over a decade. (Australia, incidentally, was one of South Africa's main supporters, possibly fearing that a debate on apartheid could lead eventually to a debate on the treatment of Australia's Indigenous peoples.)

Countries rarely try to use the Article 2 (7) argument nowadays. China tried to claim that its human rights policies are internal affairs, but received little support – and lost the right to hold the 2000 Olympics partly because of its well-publicised poor human rights record. Thanks to the global mass media, the whole world was able to see the 1989 Tiananmen Square massacre.

The world has come a long way on the issue of human rights since the refusal of the UK, France and US to comment on Nazi Germany's 'internal affairs'.

Tensions between different types of human rights

There's an active discussion going on about the future of human rights. No one is opposed to human rights as such; rather it's a matter of what rights are to be emphasised. The dispute derives from the traditional distinction between two types of human rights, and which of the two types should get priority: civil and political rights or economic, social and cultural rights.

Many western human rights groups define 'human rights' in terms of civil and political rights. Freedom House, a New York-based group, for example, carries out an annual survey of so-called 'free' countries that is based on civil and political rights and pays little attention to economic and social rights. According to its calculations, about 60 per cent of the world's population now live in free or partly free societies.

Some developing countries are sceptical of this approach. Their societies aren't necessarily derived from the cult of the rugged individual; instead, they may be based on the family as the basic unit of society and so have a preference for cooperation rather than competition. Such countries may have a greater intervention by the government in the economic and social affairs of the country, and resent being told how to conduct their affairs by human rights groups and western governments that come from a different tradition.

My view is that more attention needs to be given to emphasising how much each category of human rights needs the other. There's no automatic distinction between them. Western countries themselves have traditions of cooperation and the sharing of property. They also helped pioneer economic and social rights, such as education and health; they began the 'welfare state' about a century ago.

Additionally, the western model of economic development isn't necessarily easily applied by other countries. Some of the west's wealth has been derived from exploiting what are today's developing countries. Developing countries don't have their own colonies to exploit.

The difficulties confronting countries vary from one country to the next. There is, for example, a mismatch in population and land. China and India represent almost 40 per cent of the world's population but have only 10 per cent of the earth's surface. Canada, New Zealand and Australia occupy about another 10 per cent of the earth's surface but have less than 1 per cent of the world's population.

Economic wealth remains badly distributed. The 30 per cent of the world's population who live in developed countries own 85 per cent of the world's wealth. The vast majority of humankind therefore only owns 15 per cent. That's not so very different from the situation during the heyday of the great empires in the sixteenth to nineteenth centuries.

Meanwhile, civil and political rights can contribute to economic and social development. For centuries, the burden of running the world, of providing the expertise for scientific and technological progress and of providing the artistry for culture has been carried by a minority of the world's population: white men. Civil and political rights guarantee the full involvement of all people in national and international affairs. The world's destiny will be decided by all races and both sexes. Men in Africa, Asia and Latin America and women around the world are only beginning their involvement in shaping the world's destiny. There is a vast amount of brainpower yet to be tapped.

A greater respect for civil and political rights should reduce the need for spending money on armed forces, police and intelligence services, because a government will have less fear of domestic rebellion. More money can then be made available for economic and social development.

'Open societies' have for centuries made more economic and social progress than 'closed societies', because of the free flow of ideas. If that flow is hindered and everything is derived from a single source instead, stagnation sets in. Economic growth doesn't come from the barrel of a gun.

Consequently, it's important that the advocates of each type of human rights recognise how much one type of human rights helps the other.

Rosa Parks: A woman who changed the United States

The Civil Rights Movement not only changed the United States; it also inspired similar activities in other countries, including Australia. The Reverend Doctor Martin Luther King Jnr was well known as the leader of the Civil Rights Movement, but we also know more now about the woman who triggered his interest in the need to end racism: Rosa Parks.

The Civil Rights Movement began on the evening of Thursday, 1 December 1955 on Cleveland Avenue, Montgomery, Alabama. Rosa Parks, aged forty-two, an African American seamstress employed by a Montgomery department store, boarded a bus and sat in the 'coloured' section at the back. Buses – like the rest of Montgomery – were segregated. Black passengers paid their fare at the front door, reserved for whites, then walked to the black entry at the back. Sometimes drivers would accept the fare then drive off while a passenger was walking alongside the bus to the rear entry.

Rosa Parks had no intention of becoming one of America's heroes. She was simply tired of the racism and the second-class status. When a young white man boarded the crowded bus and demanded her seat, Rosa Parks refused to move. The bus driver called the police, who arrested, fingerprinted and gaoled Rosa Parks. She was released on bail, and four days later was found guilty of disorderly conduct and fined US$14.

Some black congregation members at the Baptist Church of the Reverend Doctor Martin Luther King Jnr formed the

Montgomery Improvement Association to begin a campaign to end the local segregation – and eventually to end the institutional racism throughout the United States. King was twenty-six and had only just begun his religious career. He became the leader of the boycott because he was the newest minister in town and hadn't yet made many enemies.

The Montgomery Improvement Association spearheaded a black boycott of the bus company. About three-quarters of the passengers were black, so this represented a major loss of revenue for the company. Meanwhile, the legality of the bus segregation rule went through the legal system, and on 13 November 1956 the US Supreme Court ruled the segregation to be unconstitutional. The boycott ended on 20 December 1956, 381 days after the conviction of Mrs Parks, when Dr King was convinced that the bus company would honour the Court's ruling.

Dr King went on to even greater glory, including winning the Nobel Peace Prize. It's a matter of speculation as to what role he would have played in the Civil Rights Movement if the incident hadn't taken place – if Rosa Parks had sat further back in the bus, or if she'd missed that particular bus entirely. No doubt the momentum of the Civil Rights Movement would have been built up through other causes, but it may not have included Dr King in the leading role.

And what happened to Rosa Parks? She was sacked from her seamstress job in January 1956, and she and her husband, Raymond, were constantly harassed and threatened. In 1957, they moved to Detroit to live near Rosa's younger brother Sylvester. She resumed her work as a seamstress, and in 1965 got a receptionist job working for a black member of the US Congress, John Conyers, where she stayed until her retirement in September 1988. Raymond died in 1977 from cancer.

In recent years, with the upsurge of interest in both the history of the Civil Rights Movement and the role of women generally in US history, we've learned a great deal more about Rosa Parks.

She was born Rosa Louise McCauley in Tuskegee, Alabama, on 4 February 1913. Her father, James, was a carpenter and her mother, Leona, was a teacher. She married Raymond Parks, a barber, in December 1932. Rosa was aware right from childhood of the dangers that all black people had to endure. As a girl, she heard the Ku Klux Klan riding at night to a lynching and feared her own house would be burned down. She became a member of the African Methodist Episcopal Church, which in the pre-Civil War days was called the 'Freedom Church' because of its campaign to end slavery.

In February 1987, nearing retirement, she formed the Rosa and Raymond Parks Institute for Self-Development, to educate black youths to be inspired about the history and heritage of the Civil Rights Movement and to work harder for their own advancement. It was only late in life that the honours started to arrive: people were at last recognising the 'her-story' of the Civil Rights Movement. In 1996, Rosa Parks was awarded the Presidential Medal of Freedom and in 1999 the Congressional Gold Medal. Cleveland Avenue in Montgomery, Alabama, where she stood up for racial equality by remaining sitting down, is now called Rosa Parks Boulevard.

45

❓ What progress has been made in the international protection of human rights?

International Human Rights Day is commemorated on 10 December each year, the anniversary of the UN General Assembly's adoption in 1948 of the Universal Declaration of Human Rights. This is the basic document of the global human rights revolution. It was adopted with no votes against it, but there were some abstentions. The Soviet Union and its East European allies abstained because the Declaration contained the right to own property; South Africa opposed the principle that all races were equal; and Saudi Arabia opposed the principle that women were equal to men.

The progress of the global human rights revolution can be seen through the changes in these countries. Communism has collapsed in Eastern Europe and people can now own property there; apartheid has gone in South Africa and the country now has an African president. Only the sexism in some Islamic thinking is still current.

Human rights are part of the political vocabulary

One of the achievements of the global rights revolution is that political claims are expressed in terms of 'human rights'. Even if people are unfamiliar with the details of the UN's declarations and treaties, there is widespread interest in human rights, and people are more likely than ever before to oppose abuses of governmental power that violate human rights. People are still being treated badly, but they know their rights are being violated. People are not dying in ignorance.

Flow-on declarations and treaties

The UN has produced a diverse range of declarations and treaties flowing from the 1948 Declaration, such as the 1966 covenants on civil and political rights and economic, social and cultural rights (to which Australia is a party). These, plus the Declaration, constitute the basic 'international bill of rights'.

Other important treaties include:

- 1951 Convention on the Prevention and Punishment of the Crime of Genocide, which provides for the prosecution of anyone charged with commissioning acts intended to destroy, in whole or in part, a national, ethnic, racial or religious group.

- 1969 International Convention on the Elimination of All Forms of Racial Discrimination, which prohibits discrimination and the dissemination of ideas based on racial superiority or hatred.
- 1981 Convention on the Elimination of All Forms of Discrimination Against Women, which addresses discrimination in public life, education, employment, health, marriage and the family.

Assisting governments to protect human rights

The UN is also creating a network of techniques to assist governments to protect human rights. For example, UN officials have helped the new governments in Eastern Europe to devise electoral reforms.

We're also seeing the spread of the UN's work to the regional level. The best example is the Council of Europe (which contains virtually all of Europe's countries), which is doing particularly good work on civil and political rights. The Council's human rights machinery has the power to coerce member-governments to change their policies or risk expulsion from the Council.

Providing opportunities for NGOs to fight for human rights

The UN has provided an opportunity for NGOs to lobby governments to improve their human rights records. Some countries do make private requests to other governments to improve their human rights policies, but diplomatic limitations restrict any public condemnation. Non-governmental organisations (NGOs), such as Amnesty International and the International Commission of Jurists, aren't so restrained in what they can say or do.

Governments come and go, and the media can lose interest in issues, but NGOs keep on keeping on. They provide a high level of continuity for an issue. For example, the International Commission of Jurists has kept alive the issue of the deaths of journalists from Australian media outlets during the 1975 Indonesian invasion of East Timor. NGOs also kept alive the allegations against General Pinochet and the human rights violations in Chile, and eventually European governments decided they had to act in response to this continuing public concern. Nowadays, dictators can run but they can't hide.

46

❓ How serious is the United States' national debt problem?

The worst debtor in world history is the US Government. The current size of the US national debt is almost US$7 trillion (that is, 7 million million American dollars) – a sum of money beyond the understanding of most people. As an example, let's say a person spent US$1 million per day every day since Jesus was born, then it would take until around the year 2737 to spend just the first trillion dollars. The US National Debt is about seven times that amount.

The debt consists of all the obligations of the US Treasury to pay money to the US Government's creditors (see 'The Debt to the Penny' www.publicdebt.treas.gov/opd/opdpenny.htm and 'US National Debt Clock' www.brillig.com/debt_clock). The US Treasury permits patriotic Americans to make donations to pay off the debt;

cheques are to be made to the Bureau of Public Debt in West Virginia.

The US began the 1980s as the world's major lending country. It ended the 1980s as the world's main borrowing country. In the meantime, Japan became the world's largest creditor country and has financed a third of the US national debt. Debt has destroyed empires in the past, and it's now a major problem for the US.

The US has always had a national debt. The first version was created at the outset of the American War of Independence against the British (1776–83). As soon as the fighting started, the Continental Congress authorised the issue of US$2 million worth of bills of credit (called Continentals) to finance the war. An old American expression to describe something that's useless, 'It's not worth a Continental', derives from 1780, when the Continental Congress issued too many Continentals and created the worst bout of inflation in US history. The new country had a very poor international credit rating because foreigners thought the Americans couldn't handle their finances properly.

The British were eventually driven out in 1783. Under the original Constitution, the new US Government didn't have any independent power to raise revenue. Meanwhile, the thirteen states had their own debts to pay off and were reluctant to provide money to the new government. The new country started to slide into chaos: the government was broke and the individual states were squabbling among themselves. In 1787, there was a conference in Philadelphia to create a better Constitution and a stronger national government. That 1787 Constitution gave the US Government the power to tax. It remains in force today and is the international benchmark for national constitutions.

The current form of national debt was started in 1791

and it was US$75 million. This may seem a small amount of money now but it represented about 40 per cent of the US's gross national product. The national debt has tended to keep growing. It reached a new high in 1804 when the US Government bought the Louisiana territory off France (the 'Louisiana Purchase') for US$11.25 million.

Thomas Jefferson, the third US President and one of the authors of the new Constitution, hated owing money. He knew a lot about it because in 1773 he had inherited from his father-in-law an estate burdened with debt. Jefferson believed that creating a national debt would serve only to enrich 'the tribe of bank-mongers . . . seeking to filch from the public their swindling and barren gains', but the Louisiana Purchase was too good to miss – and it has been justified by history. So national debt is not necessarily a bad thing, provided the money is used for worthwhile projects.

In the 1830s, the national debt went down to its lowest level ever: US$37,513. This was due both to President Andrew Jackson being very frugal and to the US Government selling off land for development purposes.

Generally speaking, the US national debt has gone down in times of peace and up in times of war. It increased by twenty-one times in World War I and by six times in World War II. The longest sustained period of debt reduction occurred after the end of the Civil War in 1865–93, when the US Government ran a budget surplus every year and cut the debt to about a third of its initial value. This resulted in more money in circulation for private expenditure and so contributed to the booming US economy. By the beginning of the twentieth century, all this growth meant that the US had become one of the world's main economies.

The Depression of the 1930s was another turning point because the national debt increased dramatically even though there was no war. The US Government was spending its way out of the Depression, such as through the creation of roads and other public works. Then came all the financial problems of World War II: the national debt in 1946 was 128 per cent of gross national product.

After the war, the US embarked upon its biggest period of economic growth – as did most of the rest of the world. For two years during the eight years of the Eisenhower Government in the 1950s, the US Government even ran at a surplus. The national debt was slightly reduced.

But from the 1960s, US governments started to fall back into increasing the national debt. The Vietnam War, for example, was politically unpopular and couldn't be financed from traditional methods such as compulsory saving and increased taxation, so the government borrowed to pay for it.

The Reagan Administration (1980–88) embarked upon the largest and most expensive peacetime military expansion in US history. President Reagan, who, ironically, was committed to reducing US Government budget deficits, borrowed more than all his predecessors combined. In the middle of 1985 – despite the economic recovery then under way – the US became a net debtor internationally for the first time in seventy years.

A great achievement of the Clinton Administration (1992–2000) was the balancing of the federal budget. By this time the Cold War was over and President Clinton was reluctant to get the US involved in further wars. Additionally, the US economy was booming again and so the government was doing well from taxation. In the late 1990s, Clinton was speculating on what could be done about the first lot of budget surpluses since the Eisenhower Administration.

The Clinton Administration ran four consecutive budget surpluses and in May 2000 Clinton announced the largest paydown on the national debt in US history. The national debt was US$2.4 trillion lower than it was projected to be when he entered office in 1992. Clinton predicted that the US could 'pay off the entire national debt by 2013 for the first time since Andrew Jackson was President'.

That optimism has now gone. The current President Bush has increased the annual government deficits by both introducing tax cuts and raising defence expenditure. The War on Terrorism and the cost of rebuilding Iraq are adding to the national debt. The US Government is now back to record annual government budget deficits and the largest national debt in world history.

We hear a lot about the Third World 'debt crisis'. But another crisis is the US's own national debt. After World War II, the Americans reined in Britain. Now China – the emerging economic superpower and an American creditor – may have to rein in the US and instruct it to stop living on credit and start living responsibly.

47

What is the 'Fourth World'?

The First World was the US and its allies (including Australia); the Second World was the Soviet Union and its allies; and the vast Third World comprised all the developing countries that wished to be neutral between those two power blocs. The Fourth World refers to the minority populations within nation-states. The UN has been very successful with its decolonisation process. But there is a new set of problems arising from some of the minority populations within countries. Indeed, the formal decolonisation process is now being followed by 'colonial' problems of different types.

Economic neocolonialism

Formal colonialism may have ended but the economies of most developing countries are still influenced by the terms of trade laid down during colonial times. Most still export raw materials and have to import manufactured goods from the developed world. They've borrowed heavily to pay for their development programs and are now repaying as interest to foreign banks more money than they receive from foreign aid. Developing countries are actually helping development in the developed countries. Meanwhile, they are hindered from concentrating fully on their own development issues.

Tribal problems

The European imperial process divided people into a patchwork of colonies and often split tribes into separate nationalities. In Africa, for example, rivers were perceived as a type of highway and people of the same tribe lived on either side of them. When the European map-makers appeared, they often used rivers as boundary lines on their maps, so dividing a system of tribes into colonies. The colonies eventually became independent but the old tribal boundaries weren't revived. Consequently, Africa has had tribal problems as people come to terms with the new set of dividing lines.

Internal colonisation

Some parts of the world are independent countries but have their own form of 'internal colonisation', whereby the original inhabitants of the land are treated poorly. It's these indigenous peoples who are sometimes referred to as the Fourth World.

Many developed countries also have a 'fourth world'. For example, Australia is having to come to terms with the suffering inflicted on its Indigenous people, and there are similar problems in many other countries. The UN estimates there are 300 million indigenous people in at least 5000 groups spread across the world in more than seventy countries.

Despite their diversity, they face similar problems. Most of India's tribal people live below the poverty line, and the life expectancy of indigenous people in northern Russia is eighteen years less than the national average. Two decades ago, the Brazilian government set aside a portion of land – the equivalent size of Portugal – for Indians to live on their own. Now gold and oil have been discovered there, and miners are invading the land, killing the Indians and going after the resources.

But indigenous peoples are starting to fight back. The 500-year nightmare of colonialism is coming to an end. They have survived and their numbers are slowly increasing.

Indigenous peoples are learning the strength of networking. For example, the Inuit (wrongly called 'Eskimos') who live in northern Russia, Canada and Scandinavia are sharing their experiences, including how to lobby their governments and how to mobilise the mass media. In the US, there are now 600 Native American lawyers working for their people. They also have their first senator.

They're also seeking economic compensation. For example, the annual market of pharmaceutical products derived from medicinal plants discovered by indigenous peoples exceeds US$43 billion, but the profits are rarely shared. Now indigenous peoples are campaigning for their royalty payments.

The Australian mass media coverage of the debate over Indigenous land rights created the impression that Australia alone was having to give due recognition to its Indigenous people. In fact, about sixty-nine other countries are going through the same process or will need to in the future.

48

? Which country is likely to replace the United States as the next superpower?

History never stops. The Mediterranean is the ocean of the past, the Atlantic is the ocean of the present and the Pacific is the ocean of the future.

Do China and India represent the new emerging great powers? If we apply the Kennedy cycle theory (see 'Will the US end up as just another tourist attraction?'), we can see that both are concentrating on trade and economic development, rather than military might. China enjoys a very healthy trade surplus vis-à-vis the US. Is it getting ready to replace the US as the world's major trading country?

Since World War II, the US's major trading partners have also been its main military partners. The fact that China is a major trading partner for the US, but not also a military partner, has created a breach in this setup.

The rise of China is overwhelming the rest of the world. On military matters, China is mainly concerned with internal unity – such as Tibet and putting down domestic critics – and intimidating Taiwan. It will be interesting to see how it evolves as a major military power projecting its influence overseas. However, this may be some time off if it wants to concentrate on accumulating economic wealth first.

China's rapid growth causes a problem for Australia regarding its foreign policy tradition. If the US decides to back Taiwan against China, it's likely to call on Australia to help out, which puts Australia in a difficult position as China is one of our major trading partners.

As the years roll by, however, the US won't be able to afford to stand up to China. Taiwan will become increasingly vulnerable to Chinese pressure because of its international isolation, and Australia's dilemma over its tradition of always supporting the US will increase.

49

❓ What is 'citizenship'?

'Citizenship' is one of the oldest ideas in politics but there's little international agreement about what it actually means. For example, there's no international law governing how a foreign-born settler may acquire the citizenship of another country.

At one end of the spectrum, there's the role of heritage and forebears. For example, under German law, a person of German descent living in another country has a right to claim German citizenship even though he or she has not previously lived in Germany. Meanwhile, many Turkish 'guest workers', who do much of the dirty and dangerous work in Germany, aren't given German citizenship even though they may have lived for two or three generations in Germany as taxpayers.

France takes a more middle-of-the-road approach. It defines its citizens as the inhabitants of a French territory.

This is based on the notion that being 'French' is associated with French language and culture. These can be learned and so migrants are assimilated.

At the other end of the spectrum are the US and Australia. Citizenship is acquired by residence in these countries and according to immigration criteria (such as the person's skills or whether the person has relatives already living in the country). Distant history, ethnic origins and culture don't count; what's important is a desire to flourish in the new land – and to help the land flourish in exchange.

There are still some major differences between the American and Australian approaches. The Americans, after their War of Independence (1776–83), saw themselves as new people in the New World. They wanted to get rid of old European ideas and start afresh. Most Europeans at that time were 'subjects': people governed by a king or queen. The Americans proudly proclaimed themselves to be 'citizens' of a new republic – an idea taken from Classical Greece and Rome. Civics and citizenship education have always been important in American schools, as part of the process of creating American citizens. Schoolchildren know the US Constitution, the words of the national anthem and salute the flag each day.

Just over a century later, in the 1890s, when the Australians were writing their Constitution, they deliberately avoided the issue of citizenship. They wanted to keep the document as simple as possible to get agreement on it, and thought the word 'citizenship' hinted at republicanism, independence from Britain and the removal of the royal family. Although there was a republican movement in Australia at the time, there was no great support for it. Australia was part of the British empire and all the people in the empire were 'British subjects'. There were no New Zealand or Canadian 'citizens', for example, either.

There was also the problem over the 'white Australia' policy. The British empire was the world's most multicultural empire – Queen Victoria, via her reign over India, Pakistan and Bangladesh, Egypt and the Sudan, governed a larger number of Muslims than any other person in history. The British Government didn't agree with the Australian colonial racist policy. It liked Asian workers; for instance, it recruited British Indians to work in the South Pacific and East African colonies in the belief that they were better workers than the local people. Additionally, the American Civil War had taken place only four decades earlier and London hoped to avoid any race-based civil war in the empire, wanting it to operate as one vast happy family with freedom of movement for its subjects.

But the Australian colonies wanted to remain free to impose discriminatory laws in the areas of immigration and employment. This meant not only reducing the numbers of Aborigines but also keeping out Asians and Africans. The target included the existing Chinese residents, who numbered about 36,000 at the time of Federation. The colonies didn't want to give non-whites the freedom of movement to enter Australia and the best way to solve all these problems was to avoid them. That's why there is no definition of Australian 'citizenship' in the Constitution.

After World War II there was a global shortage of labour and fewer British people wanted to migrate. Australia couldn't get enough people from Britain and so it had to recruit from other countries, mainly in Europe. This reopened the old questions over citizenship. The Canadians had already begun to create Canadian citizens and so Australia followed their lead with the Australian Citizenship Act in 1948. Since the Australian Citizenship Act came into effect, over 3 million settlers have become Australian citizens. Over 70,000 settlers continue to become new citizens each year.

50

? How does Australia rank internationally in terms of the 'good life'?

Those of us who live in the small minority of developed western countries – about 10 per cent of the world's population – shouldn't assume that what we see here is what is to be seen in the rest of the world. We are living on islands of wealth in a sea of squalor.

Australia is a very lucky country. It used to be even luckier. In 1900, Australia probably had the world's number one economy. A century later, in 2000, with many more countries now in existence, Australia was ranked at number fourteen. This is still a very high ranking, given all the twentieth century's turmoil and changes.

Why has Australia slipped down the international league table? In 1900, we sold what the world wanted: food, gold and wool. But as a person's income increases, so a smaller proportion of that income is spent on food and much more money goes on housing, furniture, holidays and other services. Therefore, it's necessary for a country to change its production focus to maintain economic growth.

Australia's tourist industry

When I first arrived in Australia from Great Britain in 1973, I was, like most newcomers, overwhelmed by the beauty of Sydney Harbour. In the first radio interview I ever did (also in 1973) I commented that Australia could do more to create a tourist industry to bring in foreign travellers. But I was told Australians were too 'Bolshevik' to be servile and that the tourist industry would never flourish here because ordinary Australians lacked the graciousness to be polite. They were also too unionised to be efficient: the unions were too powerful and could prevent new industries developing and the establishment of new flexible working hours.

In fact, in only three decades Australia has become a world leader in the international travel business. Tourism is now a major source of foreign revenue.

By contrast, unions have lost their powerful status in Australian life. Where once they were perceived as obstacles to Australia's economic development – and referred to with hatred in the media – now transnational corporations are seen as the sinister power lording it over governments. Corporation CEOs have replaced trade union bosses as the figures of popular hatred.

Australia's ranking in the Human Development Index

The United Nations Development Programme (UNDP) carries out an annual survey of the UN's main members (177 countries). In the 2004 edition of the *Human Development Report*, Australia was ranked third in the Human Development Index. The top five, in order, are: Norway, Sweden, Australia, Canada, the Netherlands. The United States came in eighth, and Britain twelfth. The bottom five countries are: Burundi, Mali, Burkina-Faso, Niger and Sierra Leone.

The Human Development Index measures the quality of life based on four important capabilities. These are the capability to:

1. Lead a strong and healthy life.
2. Be knowledgeable.
3. Have access to the resources needed for a decent standard of living.
4. Participate in the life of the community.

This is a more sophisticated measurement than simply a survey of wealth, such as an assessment of the gross national product (GNP). A country may do well in terms of the overall size of its economy but this doesn't necessarily mean that all its citizens are doing well. For example, the US has the world's largest GNP but life expectancy for a child in the US is about the same as in Cuba, one of the world's poorest countries.

The UNDP annual survey shows that life in Australia – internationally speaking – is a lot better than many Australians seem to believe. It's not true (as I sometimes hear people say) that 'the rich are getting richer and the poor are getting poorer'. In fact, the overall standard of living is going up in Australia: the rich are getting richer, and the poor are getting richer too, but at a slower rate. It's true that the gap between the rich and the poor is getting wider, but the poor are still getting richer.

Few Australian homes fifty years ago had the modern conveniences we now take for granted, for example cars, televisions, overseas holidays and telephones. Even children carry around their own mobile phone these days. The grinding poverty that characterised the lives of many Australians fifty years ago has gone.

That said, not every Australian has benefited from Australia's economic growth. Jobless families are raising almost 20 per cent of the country's children under fifteen, which means many children are growing up with no role models of adults in employment. For these families, even the basic necessities of life are a struggle. Charities that used to specialise only in foreign aid are now providing breakfasts for children in Australian schools to prevent them fainting from hunger in class.

We have seen an Americanisation of Australia: a shift from the traditional egalitarian Australian society to one with a growing gap between rich and poor. 'Two Australias' are now emerging.

It's interesting to note that the two countries ahead of Australia in the UNDP Index – Norway and Sweden – have a different approach to Australia on taxation. They take a 'social wage' approach. In other words, instead of the 'user pays' mentality in Australia, with lower taxes and individuals having to pay for whatever they want, these countries have maintained a policy of high personal taxation, which then finances a variety of social services – university education, for example. An individual has less take-home cash in his or her pay packet but can expect more services.

The 'detribalisation' of Australian politics

Australia has never been richer – and this creates new dynamics within the political parties. Australian politics has traditionally been divided into two main tribes: Liberal and Labor (with some votes going to marginal parties). But something odd is happening in politics. The old labels no longer apply – people are leaving their tribes.

Some Liberals are disgusted by the Howard Government's handling of foreign policy. Some of the biggest personal criticisms of Prime Minister Howard have come from members of the 'establishment', if not members (or ex-members) of his own party.

In August 2004, the 'Group of 43' – comprising ex-military and ex-diplomats, led by former chief of the defence force General Peter Gration – issued a public statement criticising the government's foreign and defence policy. They said that Australia is no safer as a result of its involvement in Iraq, and that involvement required it to act contrary to the UN's recommendations. This type of statement is unprecedented and indicates an erosion of trust in John Howard among the elite, the Liberal Party's traditional base.

But there is an even greater change occurring in the Labor 'tribe'. Trade unions have traditionally been Labor's main source of financial support, but now less than 25 per cent of the workforce belong to a trade union. Thanks to globalisation and the reform process initiated by the Hawke and Keating Labor Governments in the 1980s, many of Australia's traditional factory jobs have disappeared. People in the newer industries (such as computing) don't bother to join unions. The unions have a poor image – fat, old, anti-feminist men looking after themselves – and young people, particularly women, aren't interested in joining such men's clubs. Now Labor has to look to business for support and so needs to be careful about its policies affecting business.

These days, Australia is largely a middle-class country. Many people may have a working-class background or occupation but they have middle-class aspirations. For example, they have fewer children but live in much larger homes – 'McMansions' – than those they grew up in. Like the middle class everywhere, they value stability and steadiness; they're not interested in lofty visions and high-minded idealism. They have an almost apolitical attitude: provided they're doing well out of the economy, they're not much interested in what is happening in politics.

The Labor Party has been a victim of its own success. Its policies over the decades have helped lift many poor Australians out of poverty, but they're ungrateful. They're now more inclined to vote Liberal than Labor, because they have some wealth to protect – from 'boat people', for example. In the past, communities would work together to confront common problems, such as the Depression. Now it's everyone for themselves; there's no longer any sense of working-class solidarity. People aren't willing to share their wealth with others.

Australia's low levels of corruption and crime

Australia also shows up well in the annual survey carried out by Transparency International, a Berlin-based international non-government organisation that compiles an annual

Corruption Perception Index. This is a poll of polls, reflecting the perceptions of businesspeople and country analysts.

In the 2004 index, Australia came in at ninth position, out of 146 countries. Ahead of Australia were Finland, New Zealand, Denmark, Iceland, Singapore, Sweden, Switzerland and Norway. The UK was eleventh and the US was seventeenth. The bottom five countries were Chad, Myanmar, Nigeria, Bangladesh and Haiti.

Despite what the politicians may claim during election campaigns, Australia is a reasonably safe place to live. It has a low murder rate – nineteen murders per every 1 million people – which has hardly changed over the 100 or so years since national records began. It is a much better rate than the US at 63, Russia at 210 and South Africa at 560.

One of the reasons Australia does so well out of Japanese tourism is that the Japanese feel safe here. Japan's murder rate is one of the lowest in the world. More Japanese would like to visit the US but they see it as a dangerous place: there's a higher murder rate of Japanese in the US than there is among the Japanese in Japan.

The right indicators

Over the years, various benchmarks have been developed to identify 'successful' countries. Some of the best-known indicators include:

- an ability to feed the country's population
- large reserves of natural resources
- an educated workforce
- stable government
- no predatory enemies over the border trying to invade the country.

On this basis, Australia certainly has the right indicators to be a 'successful' country.

Australia has a lot more going for it than many Australians seem to realise. Indeed, I find that the main source of negative opinion about Australia comes from Australians themselves. Foreigners have a much higher opinion of this country.

Australians, therefore, are very fortunate. But to whom much is given, a great deal is expected, and so we should not take our fortunate position for granted. The world is undergoing a large amount of change. We need to keep up to date with world affairs and ensure that Australia's policies are relevant for the new era.

We also need to keep ourselves informed about the future. After all, that is where we are going to spend the rest of our lives.

Acknowledgements

I have very much enjoyed writing this book and have been most impressed with the speed and efficiency of the Random House team.

In particular I would like to thank Channel 7 *Sunrise* viewer Jude McGee, Publisher at Random House, for first suggesting the idea for the book.

Sophie Ambrose, Managing Editor, and Nicola O'Shea, Editor, were also very important to help the book proceed through all the stages.

My thanks to all three people.